SILENT SHAME

SILENT SHAME

The Alarming Rise of Child Sexual Abuse
and How to Protect Your Children from It

Martin Mawyer

CROSSWAY BOOKS • WESTCHESTER, ILLINOIS
A Division of Good News Publishers

First printing, 1987

Printed in the United States of America

Library of Congress Catalog Card Number 86-72062

ISBN 0-89107-419-8

CONTENTS

To my wife, Bonnie, and our children, whose patience, support, and sacrifice made this book possible.

Special Thanks: Dr. Jerry Falwell and Dr. Ronald Godwin, who allowed me to travel and research this important topic; William Willoughby, who imparted his laudable journalistic skills to me, at his *own* cost; Marie Layne, whose proofreading skills are invaluable; my special friend John Whitehead, whose encouragement and professional counseling (and his many prayers) have made this project a success.

ONE

A NATION ALARMED

Meredith S.—a twice convicted child molester—suddenly stopped telling his most shocking story of child sexual abuse. Noticing my paralytic look, he cocked a half-embarrassed smile and asked, "You're not going to let this stuff get to you, are you? I mean, if you're not careful this stuff will destroy your faith in the human race."

Inwardly I shook off my numbness and told Meredith I was doing fine. But as I sat in a cold and barren "holding room" at Powhatan Correctional Center in Powhatan, Virginia, listening to his stories of abduction, seduction, beatings, molestings, and near killings, I continued to be haunted by mental paralysis.

Quite frankly—after I had spent a year of intense investigation into child sex abuse—Meredith S. and his cohorts *were* beginning to dismember my "faith in the human race."

How to Have Sex with Kids, What Is Pedophilia Anyway?, Children and Sadomasochism—all were written by David Sonenschein, forty-three, a seemingly trustworthy employee at the Austin Independent School District in Austin, Texas.[1]

These sex manuals, brought to public attention by a television reporter in July 1984, also revealed that Sonenschein was a pedophile: a person who is sexually attracted to young children. The manuals, graphically written, told pedophiles how to meet children, how to keep a relationship secret, and how to persuade children to have anal, oral, vaginal, masturbatory, and group sex.

In one chapter, "Meeting Kids," Sonenschein tells the pedophile how to use jobs, friends, and other children to meet new kids—and avoid parents. "After you get to know each other and start having a sexual relationship, you can go to unknown and secret places. . . . It is a good idea to get to know parents. Sometimes you can get baby-sitting tasks or you can just take the kids places when they (the parents) know you and know that the kids like being with you. Sometimes parents can introduce you to other kids, too."

Defending these activities, Sonenschein wrote: "The point is, none of it is 'sick' or 'sinful' or 'inappropriate.' It all ought to be just fun where nobody owes anybody and no one direction is best."

Authorities also learned that Sonenschein is listed as associate editor of a newsletter published by the Childhood Sexuality Circle, a group that actively promotes the legalization of sex between adults and children.

Upon discovery of these sex manuals, Sonenschein was fired from his job in the school district's student records division.

Fired or not, troubling questions remained: How many pedophiles are there in the United States? How well organized are they? Do they really have tested and proven strategies for disarming parents and seducing children? Are they actually volunteering for jobs as youth leaders? Do they really view their activities as legitimate?

But if Sonenschein is just one of tens of thousands . . .

Experts now know Sonenschein *is* only one of thousands, perhaps a hundred thousand pedophiles—perhaps even more—in America. But what experts have known for several years, the public has only recently begun to learn. Two dramatic cases have changed all that.

The "Kiddie Porn Queen"

The first case involved Catherine Stubblefield Wilson—the nation's so-called "kiddie porn queen" from Los Angeles.[2] Though living off a welfare check, Mrs. Wilson was able to afford the finer things in life—a 1977 Rolls Royce, a 1977 Cadillac, a 1981 BMW, a private school for her children, and a plush Wilshire home—because Mrs. Wilson, a divorced mother of five, grossed five hundred thousand dollars a year selling and distributing (but not producing) child pornography.

After ten years of investigation, Los Angeles vice detectives raided Mrs. Wilson's home and six other locations in 1982 and seized hundreds of 8mm and 10mm films and magazines. The films included such titles as *Kindergarten Orgy, Randy Lolitas,* and *Little But Lewd.* Both films and magazines involved children—as young as six years—in sex acts with adults, children, and animals.

Mrs. Wilson took great care distributing the child pornography items. She received mail-ordered subscriptions and payments for the magazines and films from a bogus company in Denmark where an associate mailed her a coded order list. Mrs. Wilson deciphered the order list and then drove to various points in the western United States—Tucson, Las Vegas, and Reno—to mail the material.

When police raided her home they also uncovered a mailing list with more than *thirty thousand pedophile subscribers,* including subscribers from Denmark, England, and Canada. This figure is extremely alarming because statistics reveal the pedophile has an insatiable appetite for children. The average child molester has sexually abused sixty-eight children.[3] One forty-two-year-old man has admitted to molesting a thousand boys; a fifty-two-year-old man has admitted to five thousand molestations; and a sixty-two-year-old executive has admitted to molesting a boy each day for thirty years![4] Obviously, then, the thousands of pedophiles on Mrs. Wilson's mailing list could easily represent people who have abused hundreds of thousands of children in the United States.

In the summer of 1984, Mrs. Wilson—now twice convicted—was found guilty of distributing child pornography and sentenced to twenty-four years in prison.

The Trash of a Trashman

The second case involved a twice-convicted child molester, James Rud, and twenty-four other adult residents of Jordan, Minnesota, who were charged with over four hundred counts of child molesting.

Rud, a newcomer to Jordan and the first adult apprehended, pled guilty to nine charges of criminal sexual conduct. But his guilty plea was on condition that prosecutors would drop ninety-eight other pending criminal charges for his testimony against the twenty-four defendants who, allegedly, sexually molested forty children.

Those arrested included a deputy sheriff, a police officer, a county assessor, truck drivers, mechanics, secretaries, waitresses, factory workers, and several unemployed. But only Rud, a garbage collector, confessed. (And though only twenty-five adults were charged, police files indicated forty-five adults were subsequently accused by more than fifty children.)

The children (ages two to seventeen) claimed the adults (many their own parents) held games of "hide and seek." The children were required to remove their clothes, hide, and have sex with the adult who found them. Some children claimed they were filmed in obscene movies. Others said they were passed to adults at social gatherings, or forced to perform sex with each other, or forced to perform sex with animals. Pills, liquor, and threats were reportedly used to lower inhibitions and compel the children to obey.

By September 1984, in a bizarre twist to an already twisted tale, some children were claiming that up to three children, after appearing in a pornographic film, were killed by a "film maker" named Lefty Smith who had Chicago Mafia connections. These murdered children were reportedly either buried in the backyard of one defendant's home or dumped into the Minnesota River. One child told his therapist that several people during a party took a young boy "like an animal and hung him over a tub until he bled out enough to be wrapped in a canvas tarp."

But one year after prosecutors began their intense—and oftentimes heartless—investigations, many children admitted to lying—lying about children murdered, lying about sexual abuse by adults. By this time, however, the damage was done—many parents lost jobs, homes, savings, and reputations. And many had been without their children for almost a year. Even Rud, who was eventually convicted and sentenced to forty years in prison, admitted to lying when he accused the twenty-four other adults. Rud said he found offers of a "lighter sentence" enticing. And still, even though child after child admitted to fabricating their stories, state officials—rather than vindicating the adults—decided to leave a specter of guilt over their heads by saying the parents were acquitted because of poor prosecution rather than because no crime had been committed.

But the damage created by Jordan prosecutors did not end here. Since news stories of child murders and molestings—especially by a ring of adults from a traditionally conservative community—make *big* headlines and form lasting opinions, and acquittals do not, these unfortunate parents will continue to bear the public scars of being accused child molesters.[5]

A Nation Alarmed
Introduced to the apparent widespread and organized abuse of young children, the nation—quite rightfully—became alarmed.

Numerous child sex abuse cases against day-care centers made parents, who have grown quite accustomed to placing their child in the care of third-parties, suspicious of day-care workers. One expert now suggests that pedophiles are setting up day-care centers for the sole purpose of sexually exploiting children.[6]

The Cathy Wilson case told parents that thousands upon thousands of pedophiles are sitting in their homes, flipping through hideous child pornography magazines, fantasizing about how they can sexually abuse small children.

The Jordan, Minnesota, case told parents that a ring of child sex molesters can form even in an "everyday, neighborly, small town" (and self-described "Christian community") where fifty adults (out of a population of only 2,700) sexually abuse, drug, beat, and kill children.

The public attention given these, whether or not those charged have been found guilty, has filled the nation with fear, anxiety, and distrust.

Story after story now began appearing in newspapers and on the television screen dramatizing child sexual abuse and the nation's response: former Senator Paula Hawkins told a national conference that she was sexually abused by a sixty-year-old neighbor when she was but five years old. Within a week, nearly a hundred people went to Senator Hawkins and told their own stories of child sex abuse. Congress held several child pornography and sex abuse hearings. Eventually a bill was passed stiffening child obscenity laws. President Reagan blasted the "vicious" child molester as he signed the new bill into law. Television networks, besides creating special documentaries on the subject, immediately set out to produce movies exposing (or in some cases, exploiting) the problems of child sex abuse—*Something About Amelia, Kids Don't Tell, The Atlanta Child Murders, Child Sexual Abuse: What Your Children Should Know.* And a survey of 930 women in San Francisco revealed the apparent widespread abuse of girls—a frightening four out of ten said they were sexually abused before reaching eighteen years of age.[7]

There were even reports of children abusing other children. In Topeka, Kansas, police arrested a thirteen-year-old boy for molesting a four-year-old girl.[8] In Minonk, Illinois, two baby-sitters, twelve and fourteen years old, were charged with battering and sexually molesting a seven-month-old baby.[9] In St. Petersburg, Florida, a nine-year-old boy was found guilty of first-degree murder in the torture death of an eight-month-old girl. The baby, Barbara Parks, was tormented to death after the boy, and his seven-year-old brother, abused the girl with a pencil and coat hanger. The older boy was found guilty (among other charges) of three counts of sexual battery.[10]

And the fears these stories generated were further fueled by local and nationally reported discoveries of literally hundreds of other child sex abuse cases—from acts of abuse by unremarkable people to acts of abuse by community leaders and individuals from highly respected institutions.

Indeed, some very prominent organizations had trusted personnel accused or convicted of child molesting.

The Children's Theater School. John Clark Donahue, founder of this nationally acclaimed theater and school in Minneapolis, admitted to three counts of criminal sexual contact with three boys. Police accused him of bribing boys into sexual situations by telling them that he loved them and by discussing their parts in forthcoming productions. Police also charged the school's dance instructor, an actor, and a sound technician with sexual abuse of male or female students. Donahue was sentenced to one year in prison.[11]

West Point Military Academy. Parents of eleven children, ages thirteen months to three and one-half years, alleged that their children were sexually abused by day-care workers at this world-renowned military academy. The West Point Child Development Center was placed under an internal investigation and later cleared of all charges.[12]

The Nebraska School for the Deaf. Officials at this state-run school in North Platte, Nebraska, were charged with sexual abuse, sexual misconduct, and child abuse by the deputy Douglas County attorney. Besides charges of having sexual relations with children, many staff members were accused of not stopping sex between consenting minors and not protecting those unconsenting minors from sexual abuse by their peers. One male teacher, who was still on staff, had been previously convicted of having oral sex with a man in a public restroom at a shopping mall. But charges were dropped against staff members because of the constitutionality of a statute.[13]

Boy Scouts of America. Several troop leaders have been charged or convicted with child sex abuse. The most notorious incident involved a troop of forty boys that was founded for the sole purpose of providing sexual services to older men. These men would accompany the boys on outings and film the scouts in various sexual acts. Police found one Boy Scout official with five thousand child pornography pictures and slides. Some of the children pictured were as young as two years old.[14]

Boys Farm, Inc. Rev. Claudis I. "Bud" Vermilye established this home for wayward boys in southern Tennessee. Vermilye had previously left the Episcopal Church in Georgia after being accused of trying to seduce boys in his home and at church. Yet he operated this boys' home for five years before police shut it down for child sex abuse. Vermilye had the boys engage in sexual orgies with sponsors and clients of the farm who would spend a night or a weekend there. These acts were filmed and sold as a "remembrance of moments of the acts which transpired." Police found movies and more than a thousand lewd photos. A metal box was confiscated identifying 270 active and 87 inactive members.[15]

Depending on where one lives, or how well he or she scans the newspaper, a person could easily read about others indicted or convicted for child sex abuse. These include clergymen, day-care operators, baby-sitters, schoolteachers, counselors, coaches, principals, doctors, dentists, psychologists, lawyers, fathers, relatives, public officials, policemen, publicly honored citizens, judges, a YMCA volunteer, a Big Brothers and Sisters volunteer, a city Jaycees president, grocery store clerks, a vice president of an electronics firm, a dock loader, a 4H Club leader . . . The list is endless.

Shattered Trust

A cursory review of this list of trusted and respected individuals is sufficient to send tremors down the spine: How can parents hope to guard their children against sexual abuse when pedophiles have successfully infiltrated society's most notable and trustworthy institutions? A closer examination of each case—which reveals the incredible amount of time, strategy, and dedication each pedophile devotes to seducing children, and society's apparent ineffectiveness in stopping or curing the child offender—can almost traumatize even the most stouthearted.

People feel secure and safe only when they can maintain faith in society's institutions—faith that schools will prepare and educate, that day-care centers will train and nurture, that churches will inspire and discipline, that youth agencies will guide and coach, that public officials will stand as pillars and examples, that doctors will cure and restore, and that policemen will protect and preserve. How can the nation continue to operate efficiently if society believes the physician, the pastor, the teacher, the councilman, or the judge may be a child molester? And how can these fears be soothed when—almost daily now—newspapers and television broadcasters reveal yet another day-care center, school, church, or youth group that has been infiltrated by a pedophile who has sexually abused one—or maybe a dozen—boys and girls?

Children are easily victimized by adults—especially by those adults they have been taught to obey and trust. Since they are physically and mentally less developed than their predators, children are easily bribed, cajoled, or threatened to participate in illicit sex. How can parents, knowing the vulnerability of children, and knowing the necessity of society's institutions, avoid feeling shattered, powerless, abandoned, and demoralized as they discover the institutions they trusted are no longer inviolable?

Nor does the anxiety end here. Parents are also learning that pedophiles, besides infiltrating youth-oriented organizations and professions, are also pursuing children at any program or activity where youth congregate and are left unsupervised by parents, such as public swimming pools, beaches, video arcades, skating rinks, shopping malls, and parks. The nation became painfully aware of this in January 1985 when police finally found thirteen-year-old Robert Smith, Jr., who had been missing from his California home for two years. Robert, who was discovered in Scituate, Rhode Island, had been abducted on his way to school. His abductor was a man he knew who hung around a local video arcade shop and who became friends with Robert by giving him money for video games—a common strategy among pedophiles. But Robert, who was sexually abused by the man, was not the only child the pedophile abducted. Police also found photos of six other children in the man's possession—none of whom have been identified.[16]

And neither does the anxiety end here. Parents are also learning that their child may be abducted from almost under their eyes—front yards, stores, homes, even their arms. Patty and Mike Bradbury, of Huntington Beach, California, lost their three-year-old child to an abductor during a family camping trip at Joshua Tree National Monument.[17] One Bellflower, California, couple lost their child to a young woman who posed as a hospital photographer.[18] Thomas Childers, a navy man from Norfolk, Virginia, was convicted of abducting children by removing their bedroom screen window and whispering that someone was stealing their bike. When the children came to the window, Childers would grab them in his arms. The children then were taken a few blocks from their home and molested in Childers' vehicle.[19] How can parents possibly prepare and defend their children against such chicanery and entrapments?

There are still other causes of anxiety. Police investigative and law enforcement procedures have often been ineffective in child sexual abuse cases. Society still has no answers for the cause of pedophilia—much less its prevention. The medical profession has been unable to provide a cure for child molesters. Some attempted solutions raise questions about who needs the medical treatment more—the doctor or the sex offender. For example, Theodore Frank, who had been arrested on seventeen child-sex charges in twenty years, was released from California's Atascadero State Hospital because officials believed his molesting days were over. As part of his treatment, said law professor and prosecutor Irving Pager, "Frank's wife [who weighed 300 pounds] was asked to dress up as a child. She and Frank, who was small and skinny, were then supposed to have sex together so that he could work out his fantasies." Thus "treated," Frank was released from the hospital. Six weeks later Frank abducted two-year-old Amy Sue Seitz. He tortured, raped, and murdered the child.[20] Frank was then sentenced to death—a remedy more potently effective than turning a wife into a 300-pound nymphet.

Since the medical profession offers little hope for curing child sex offenders, society's refusal to deal firmly or justly with child sex offenders causes even more anxiety. Most child molesters receive suspended or light prison sentences. But imagine the horror residents in Ames, Iowa, felt when a state adjudicator ordered their junior high school to rehire Eldon Vaner Zel as a math teacher knowing the man had just been fired as a school system counselor for exposing himself to children.[21]

The Parent Police

To read headlines about child sex abuse is alarming. To read news stories about child sex abuse is depressing. But to dig deeper, to walk into the underground world of a child sex molester, to read his pornography, to know his strategy, to hear his stories, to feel his pain and the pain he has inflicted on others is to risk shattering one's faith in the dignity of mankind.

The following five chapters are more shocking than the headlines and news stories covered here. They dig deeper. The reader may wish to stop here and return to a sane world built around home, family, and work—at least the sane world that he imagines. But the child molester knows *no* boundaries and respects *no* conventions. His specialty is to destroy such fanciful illusions of security. Painful as it may be, the reader needs to be informed about the nature, strength, and objective of his child's enemies.

We may wish to depend on the efforts of others, hoping society will police the streets for us. Yet society—for the moment—does not have a system for ferreting out pedophiles or for protecting children from molesters. Each family, if the victory is to be won, must police its own streets, youth clubs, churches, schools, and entertainment centers. An informed parent who knows how the pedophile operates, his habits, his strategies—though admittedly painful and petrifying—is the surest means of protecting the nation's children from the preying hands of the molester.

In the next five chapters, the reader will learn much about pedophiles—their history, seductive techniques, lifestyles, and practices. Obviously, the reader will not be able to spot a pedophile from the look on his face. But the reader will be prepared to spot characteristics and habits unique among pedophiles. Undoubtedly the reader will sometimes suspect an innocent person of being a child molester. But after reading the following chapters, the reader will understand that such concern is both warranted and justified.

FROM THE GUTTER TO THE STREETS

Child pornography has been infecting this country for centuries. Even before the invention of the camera, children have been portrayed in lewd and lascivious acts by child pornographers in drawings, writings, and paintings.

But the camera added a new dimension to child pornography. For unlike writings and drawings, photographs required children as live models. This meant that pornography moved from demented imagination to criminal exploitation. As early as 1862 children were being photographed naked with both adults and animals.

From the beginning, child pornography has not been limited to the dregs of society. Such respected figures as Lewis Carroll (1832-98) engaged in child pornography. Mr. Carroll, who authored such child classics as *Alice's Adventures in Wonderland* and *Through the Looking Glass,* took photos of nude girls as young as six years.[1]

Finding a Common Creed

Little is known about pedophile activity during the turn of the century. Certainly pedophiles were not well organized—as they are today. And it is doubtful that they communicated with one another—as they do today. But in 1955 this subculture was provided a common creed when G. P. Putnam's Sons published the highly controversial novel *Lolita*. Written by Vladimir Nabokov, *Lolita* detailed the sexual relationship between a forty-two-year-old man, Hubert Humbert, and a twelve-year-old girl, Dolores "Lolita" Hayes.[2] Perhaps more than anything else, this novel provided pedophiles with many rationalizations favoring child sex.

For instance, according to this book, the pedophile is not really a victim of his own perversion, but a victim of a "spell" which certain girls unwittingly cast upon every man. These girls, generally between the ages of nine and fourteen, are "nymphets," and their sexual magnetism to older men is nothing more than a display of their "true nature." Not every girl is a nymphet, of course. And not every man is a pedophile. According to this book, a pedophile is a man whose genes render him defenseless against the nymphet's spell. And since only pedophiles are captured by the nymphet's bite, society cannot hope to understand how a grown man could have sex with a child. Said the book's sordid leading character, Mr. Humbert, "I found myself maturing amid a civilization which allows a man of twenty-five to court a girl of seventeen but not a girl of twelve." Complaining bitterly, he argued that American society needed to leave its traditional morals and go back to its primitive roots. He explained, "Marriage and cohabitation before the age of puberty is still not uncommon in certain East Indian provinces. Lepcha old men of eighty copulate with girls of eight and nobody minds."

On and on the book provides arguments favoring child sex.

To make a long and exhaustive story short, Mr. Humbert marries a widow, Charlotte Hayes, to gain access to her twelve-year-old daughter who is nicknamed "Lolita." The young "nymph" finds Mr. Humbert sexually appealing. (This sexual attraction, we are told, is prompted by Mr. Humbert's clean-cut jaw, muscular hand, deep sonorous voice, and broad shoulders.) But for the moment, Mr. Humbert must rely only on his imagination. ("I would manage to evoke the child while caressing the mother," he said.) When mother finally discovers that her new husband is sexually longing for her daughter (because he wrote about it in his diary) she runs out in front of a car and dies an "accidental" death—to the delight of Mr. Humbert, of course. Left alone, Mr. Humbert begins a wife/daughter relationship with Lolita. The story drags on and becomes immersed in the suffering of a pedophile who must jealously guard his school-aged nymphet from other boys. The rest of the story becomes tiresome as Lolita decides to become the sexual object of other men as well.

Though the story (in my opinion) has no socially redeeming value, it did provide child predators with common arguments and language: A "Lolita" is a female nymphet; a nymphet is a girl who wants to let her sexual feelings flow to a pedophile; a pedophile is a man who is magnetically attracted to young girls and who wants to set them free from the sexual bonds of society; and society is a repressor of sexual rights between consenting adults and children.

Pedophilia Hits the Silver Screen

Six years after publication, *Lolita* became a major Hollywood motion picture directed by Stanley Kubrick, the director of *2001: A Space Odyssey, Dr. Strangelove, Clockwork Orange,* and *The Shining.*[3] Starring such well-known Hollywood actors as James Mason, Peter Sellers, and Shelly Winters, the movie had two major deviations from the book—deviations which, unfortunately, have the effect of making the viewer more tolerant and sympathetic of pedophilia. In the movie, Lolita looks to be seventeen years old, not twelve, as in the book. And Lolita, rather than Mr. Humbert, makes the sexual overtures and passions. Played by the sultry Sue Lyon, the blonde-headed Lolita could have slithered her way through even the most armed defenses. As *New York Times* movie critic Bosley Crowther criticized, "Right away, this removes the factor of perverted desire that is in the book and renders the passion of the hero more normal and understandable."[4]

In effect, then, if a viewer's basic understanding of pedophilia comes from this movie, he would probably conclude that most pedophiles are the victims of oversexed and highly aggressive *mature* teenage girls—a greatly distorted view.

Pedophilia captured Hollywood's attention in two other critically acclaimed motion pictures: *Taxi Driver* and *Pretty Baby.* Released in 1976 by Columbia Pictures, *Taxi Driver* is a disturbing film about the social madness that lurks beneath society's veneer of sanity.[5] Though giving only passing treatment to pedophilia, the movie nevertheless accurately captures the leading cause of child sex abuse: The pedophile cares more for the child than the parent.

Following on the heels of *Taxi Driver* was Hollywood's most exploitive and inaccurate film about child sex to date: *Pretty Baby.*[6] Starring Brooke Shields as a child nymphet named Violet who works in a house of prostitution, the film presents children as a highly prized sexual attraction and possession. For instance, when the young girl, Violet, is auctioned off for her first night of sex, a room full of men cast aside all scruple and trip over themselves offering the highest bid for the twelve-year-old. This scene makes a powerful statement by showing men's lust for children as being *widespread* and *natural,* even if forbidden. Most viewers, at this point, would probably reject out-of-hand the movie's depiction of so many men desiring children. To support this viewpoint, the film moves on to present the Brooke Shields character as a sensual beauty, all along trying to force the viewer to be overtaken by her charm, mystique, and innocence. If the viewer falls prey to this trap, then he has experienced just how *natural* it is to lust after the child nymphet. And once society realizes how *natural* lusting after children is, it can hardly condemn those who fall prey. In short, the movie dramatizes the pedophiles' best arguments for child sex—he is merely the victim of the nymphet's sensual spell.

(The film's director, Louis Malle, once said in *Playboy* magazine, "When *Playboy* requested a photo that would express my personal view of eroticism, I sent a shot of my two-year-old, Justine, naked.")[7]

By 1981 many critics were denouncing the "rapidly growing number of images that make sexual objects out of little girls and legitimize their sexual abuse."[8] Among their complaints were the movie *Pretty Baby*, Calvin Klein blue jean ads, and the Broadway play *Lolita*. (Said the play's director, Jerry Sherlock, "It's a wonderful black comedy about a relationsip between a thirty-seven-year-old man and a twelve-year-old girl."[9])

The December 1983 issue of *Harper's Bazaar* magazine showed just how callous society was becoming to the sexual exploitation of children. John Camp, of the *St. Paul Pioneer Press,* described what he saw in that issue as a "little hard to believe."[10]

Detailing the magazine's editorial layout on perfume, Camp said, "The photographic article featured a young girl of six or seven, in full adult makeup. In each of the different full-color photos, her hair was elaborately styled in the manner favored by models for the sexually oriented magazines like *Cosmopolitan*. And she was nude."

Above one photo of the child, the editorial layout talked of "jasmine and gardenia for seduction with just a hint of innocence." The message being that perfume has the same innocence and seduction as a naked seven-year-old child.

By 1984 society was even becoming defensive about its right to portray children as sexual objects. In Maryland, for instance, Towson State University officials refused a request that the college remove nine nude photos of a six-year-old boy on display, including one where the boy was masturbating.[11]

Pedophiles Organize, Increase Activities

Because society has shown a willingness to accept children as sex objects, it is not surprising that pedophiles have come out of the gutter and onto the streets—forming lobbying groups, communicating with one another, and increasing their abuse of children.

The most notable of pedophile organizations are the North American Man/Boy Love Association (most frequently referred to as NAMBLA), the Rene Guyon Society, and the Childhood Sensuality Circle. Receiving less public fanfare are such groups as the Diaper Pail Fraternity and the Pedophile Information Exchange.

These organizations serve three main purposes. First, they give pedophiles a brotherhood. For instance, members of the Diaper Pail Fraternity share their sexual fantasies with one another and tell how they use bottles, diapers, and rattles to enhance their sexual enjoyment. And almost every group communicates to its members through newsletters. Second, they lobby legislatures to abolish age of consent laws. Organizational members regularly appear on television and radio and testify at legislative hearings on the need to alter laws restricting child sex. Third, they promote child sex as healthy. For example, the motto of the Rene Guyon Society is "sex before age eight, or else it's too late."

By the late seventies, all the factors for a child sexual abuse epidemic were present. Pedophile groups were becoming more visible and providing child predators with "solid" arguments favoring child sex; commercial ads displaying children as sexual playthings were on the rise; society's tolerance toward abnormal sex was expanding; and the breakdown of the traditional family was increasing. (These points will be discussed in greater detail in Chapter Seven.)

By 1984, newspapers across the country featured shocking headlines about the rise of child sexual abuse.

National statistics showed an increase of 400 percent in child sex abuse reports from 1977 to 1982. In 1984 alone there were 123,000 reported cases, a 35 percent increase over 1983 and still, says one researcher, we're only touching the "tip of the iceberg." Those states reporting the most dramatic increases were North Dakota (42 percent), Texas (50 percent), Wisconsin (82 percent), Oregon (83 percent), Missouri (100 percent), and Mississippi (126 percent!).[12]

Reports coming from California in 1984 were particularly heart-wrenching: California's State Central Registry reported that more children were being placed in foster homes for child sexual abuse than for physical abuse.[13] California's Department of Public and Social Services reported that the number of day-care centers closed for sexual abuse had increased tenfold over 1978.[14] And the University of California at Los Angeles reported an "alarming" increase in the number of children under five years who suffer from venereal disease of the throat and anus.[15]

The Pedophile's Simple Strategy

The key to the child molester's success is simple: Find children from poor home environments and do a better job at meeting their emotional and physical needs than the parent.

Convicted child molester Warren K. Mumpower described this strategy to a United States Senate committee investigating child sex abuse: "Many single parents, and married ones also, are so wrapped up in 'self' that they actually pawn their children off on the pedophile . . . to get the 'brats' out of their hair.

"I would like to relate an experience of mine involving a young neighbor girl of seven or eight. I had just come home from work on a Friday afternoon and was in my bedroom relaxing for a few minutes before starting supper for my children and myself. The girl came bursting into my room in tears. After I calmed her sobbing down to a point where she could talk, she asked if she could spend the weekend. I, of course, was curious why she wanted to spend the weekend and what was all the sobbing about. Her reply was her mom was having another of her boyfriends for the weekend and she could not bear having to get up in the middle of the night to go to the bathroom walking past her mom's room and seeing what was going on. After much caressing, cuddling, and mutual fondling in the nude, I asked her, 'What was the difference between what we just did and what your mom does?' Her response: 'I *love* you.'

"Have you hugged your kids today? If not, a child molester will!"[16]

It's that simple.

THREE

STRATEGIES OF
THE CHILD MOLESTER

The vast majority of child molesters operate near their homes and, therefore, are commonly referred to as "neighborhood pedophiles" by law enforcement officials. They are typically young (only 10 percent are over fifty years old)[1] and most have been sexually abused as children themselves (80 percent).[2] Surprisingly, pedophiles are basically passive; they seldom use force and rarely kill the children they molest.

The pedophile wraps his life around his sexual obsession: Money is earned specifically for bribes—candy, gifts, toys, drugs, alcohol, video games. Employment is found in fields that provide easy access to children—schools, amusement parks, carnivals, day-care centers, churches. Homes are sought in neighborhoods near parks, schools, recreation centers. Volunteer work is spent in programs that are youth-oriented—Boy Scouts of America, 4H Club, YMCA. Possessions are bought to attract children—sports cars, rock music, fashionable dress. Social hours are passed away in areas where youth congregate—video arcades, public swimming pools, skating rinks, beaches, parks, *churches*. And private hours are spent reading child pornography, writing diaries about their latest sexual adventure, and communicating with other pedophiles.

The typical pedophile is intelligent—an intelligence that gives him extraordinary advantage over children, parents, and law enforcement officials. They come from all walks of life and do not fit any racial, geographical, or economic mold. Warned one FBI agent: "These are not street punks. In many instances the educational level of the subjects is quite high. Many are college graduates."[3]

Tools of the Trade

The pedophile has an armory of tools useful for seducing the child: organizational skills, knowledge of child psychology, the ability to communicate and interact with children, and an understanding of how to use peer pressure, rewards, and punishment.

The child is either enticed or entrapped into having sex. The pedophile's objective is to find a child that is vulnerable to psychological needs and pressures. And that pressure can be applied in a variety of forms, depending on the needs of the child.

For instance, a child needing emotional support is provided a father's image and given both physical and emotional affection. Beginning with nonsexual meetings, the pedophile may take the child to sporting events, video arcades, movies, or ice cream shops. He may give the child money, buy him gifts, or fix his bike. He may spend hours with the child playing games, watching television, and solving problems. In other words, the pedophile gives the child all the emotional support he needs in exchange for sex. By far, this is the most frequent and effective strategy employed by pedophiles.

In another instance, the pedophile may perceive that the child is vulnerable to peer pressure. Here the child is made to feel "immature" for not wanting to have sex. The pedophile may point to his friends and show how other children are "old enough" to make an "adult decision" about sex. The pedophile will then praise his friends who perform sex and belittle the child who does not. One child commented, "I didn't want them (his friends) to think I couldn't do it." Another said, "Everybody else was doing it."[4]

Some other effective psychological pressures include the use of threats, drugs, and bribes. The pedophile may intimidate children into having sex by threatening their lives, or even their family's lives. Some pedophiles have even ritualistically killed animals to frighten children into having sex. Drugs and liquor are frequently used to lower inhibitions. Some children are bribed into sex after the pedophile provides free cigarettes, rides, food, video games, and the like. Some bribes are complicated. Said one young child, "He taught us how to distract people in a store and then steal. He told us our parents would kill us if they ever found out we had been taking . . . or if the police caught us."[5] In another instance, a doctor in a college community agreed to provide medical deferments for draftees if they masturbated in front of him.[6]

In many cases, children are seduced under very little pressure—especially when boys are the victims. Reasons vary: The child enjoys the sex. He just wants to join the "fun" of his friends. He feels the few moments of sexual attention given by the pedophile are far better than the strife found at home. He has such low self-esteem that having ten dollars to buy, say, a music album is worth the sex. These cases differ greatly from those cited above because the child is so psychologically primed for abuse that the pedophile can have sex moments after meeting the child, rather than spending weeks or months courting, enticing, or entrapping the victim.

"Many times it's a power issue," said FBI assistant director Lee Laster. "Simply the power of an adult male over a child, and the child being afraid not to do it. Not because, necessarily, he's going to be beat up. But because there's that power dominance of the adult over the child."[7]

Young children are especially vulnerable to the child molester because they are "trusting, naive about sex, easily terrified, compliant to authority figures and, because of their developmental tendency toward magical thinking, easy to trick or bribe," said one leading expert, Kee MacFarlane.[8]

Keeping children from exposing the sex ring, of course, is a major concern among pedophiles. Though a number of tactics work, all have a common objective: Make the child believe that exposure will be far worse for the child than for the pedophile. The child may fear loss of affection and good times, or fear that his or her friends will find out that he's a "queer" or she's a "whore," or they may fear bodily harm from a revenging pedophile. One child said, "He [the pedophile] said he would get some kids to beat me up if I told." Another said, "He said he had knives . . . in his kitchen drawer and in the glove compartment of the bus."[9]

The pedophile, in addition to using psychological warfare on children, also tries to pull the wool over the parent's eyes. His strategy is simple: legitimize his presence around children—befriend the neighbors, eat dinner with the parents, volunteer as a youth leader, give the child a ride to make his newspaper route easier. In cases where the child is too young, the pedophile may spend years befriending the parents as he waits for the child to grow to the desired age. Not surprisingly, parents are shocked to find this neighbor has been abusing their child: "He was a camp leader," the parent cries. "He was the grandfather of her girlfriend," the parent defends. Many neighbors even come in defense of the child molester.

How well do these pedophile strategies work? The answer is so frightening, so disturbing that it defies human comprehension. According to conservative estimates, more than five hundred thousand children a year are sexually abused—some boost that yearly total to five million children.[10]

A Case History

Are children really so vulnerable, parents so dim-sighted? The true story of Ralph will serve as the answer.

Ralph was a neighborhood pedophile who, when arrested, had fifty area boys in his sex ring. Living in a small southern city, he was clearly a stickler for details. On his home computer he recorded his sexual activities with four hundred children, mostly boys, some girls.

Ralph knew, for instance, the youngest child he ever molested (5.26 years); and the oldest (19.45); even the average age of his victims, (10.89). He recorded the average number of sex acts he performed on each child (64.48) and the number of times they ejaculated each day.

He kept a calendar showing dates and types of sex activities. In his diary he had photographs and narrative information on more than fifty victims. He kept a memoranda book summarizing the sexual activity with thirty-one.

He also listed the names of those boys who belonged to his "88 Club"—a select club that could be joined only after completing four different sex acts.

Ralph's bait for the children was no more complicated than money. He paid them for odd jobs, photography sessions, and sexual acts. Think about that: With only money as an attraction, Ralph lured almost half a thousand children to perform 25,600 sex acts.

Are children vulnerable? Are parents dim-sighted?

Ralph's episode also showed society's inability, or unwillingness, to properly deal with child sexual abuse. Ralph had been arrested for child molesting twice before. He was serving five years' probation when he met his third arrest. Just one month prior, Ralph's psychiatrist wrote his probation officer saying, "There is no indication that there has been recurrence of symptoms. I feel, therefore, that his problem remains in remission."[11]

Ralph's case is alarming: If children are willing to sell their bodies for odd jobs, if an entire neighborhood of parents is blind to the ongoings of a pedophile who is molesting fifty area children, if society is going to throw the child molester back on the streets, then with what will society fight the pedophile?

Society will only begin to control child sex abuse when it

begins to understand that the pedophile is totally consumed and overtaken by his sexual perversion. He lives to have sex with children. It's not just a sexual quirk, but a sexual obsession. When the pedophile is not sexually abusing a child himself, he is reading or viewing someone else's abuse of a child.

Child Pornography

The amount of child pornography found among pedophiles is staggering. A quick review of child pornography cases under investigation by U.S. Customs for 1984 reveals that the average pedophile has 127 different child porn items in his possession when apprehended. These include films, magazines, photos, calendars, slides, and books. The lowest possession case involved a San Diego man with twelve films and thirteen magazines. The largest was a La Paz, Indiana, man with twenty-one magazines, 223 photos, sixteen films, and two calendars.[12]

The pedophile uses child pornography for five purposes: visual stimulation, a training manual for finding and seducing children, a forum for communicating with other pedophiles, a resource for arguments justifying child sex, and a visual device to manipulate children into having sex with the offender.

(1) Visual Stimulation

Child pornography reveals the total depravity and cruelty of the pedophile. In these publications children are shown having sex with other children, anal or oral intercourse with adults, sex with animals, sex while being tortured, and having adults urinate on them. That pedophiles can become sexually stimulated by viewing these sordid photographs is itself a clear indication of their dangerous psychopathy.

Child pornography is largely produced and obtained from pornographers overseas—the Netherlands, Denmark, and Sweden. Magazines range from nine to fourteen dollars each while films run much higher, from forty to eighty dollars.

Though the publications are foreign-produced, the children are typically American. These American children are photographed by pedophiles who use the pictures for personal purposes and who later sell the pictures to foreign-based pornographers for money or free subscriptions or publications. Children are generally photographed smiling, without struggle, and apparently enjoying themselves. Most children are between eight and fourteen. But in order to prove that even very young girls can have sex with older men, one magazine boasted a photograph of a naked and *pregnant* five-year-old with the caption: "It just goes to show that everything is possible."[13]

(2) A Training Manual

Child pornography magazines are an instructional device telling the pedophile how to seduce children—a nephew, a daughter, a child next door, and others. For example, one article tells of an uncle who successfully lured his nine-year-old niece into having sex through promises of ice cream and dollhouses.[14] Such stories are numerous and they answer such questions as: How to seduce a student, a child you are baby-sitting, your daughter's best friend, children whose parents are out-of-town, or children at slumber parties, and more.

Some publications even tell the pedophile where to find children. In 1972, Los Angeles police arrested a child pornographer who produced a travel guide listing 378 places in fifty-four cities and thirty-four states where a child could be found. The publication, called *Where the Young Ones Are,* sold over seventy thousand copies, at five dollars each—in just a thirteen-month period![15]

Child pornography magazines also tell the pedophile how to obtain pleasure when molesting children. *Child Discipline* tells the pedophile how to derive sexual satisfaction from beating children.[16] *Lust For Children* informs the pedophile that a child's screams while being attacked are cries of pleasure.[17]

(3) Communicating with Other Pedophiles

Most every child pornography publication provides a "Person-to-Person" directory where readers can solicit correspondence with other pedophiles, sell photos of naked children from their personal collection, request a meeting with couples who have young children, or advertise for young girls to perform in movie productions.

Some selected classifieds include:

"Pretty mother with pretty young daughters invites inquiries from gentlemen anywhere who are interested in meeting us or in photography."[18]

"Super attractive couple with cute daughters, age ten and twelve, would like to hear from others with daughters only."[19]

"Have (photos) of little boys wearing girls' clothing."[20]

"I'd like to meet a girl or young divorcee with daughters for possible marriage."[21]

"Divorced or widowed females wanted with young children for exciting relationships."[22]

"Modern couple with eleven-year-old daughter wants contact with same."[23]

"Film studio is looking for nice young girls (preferably with long hair) up to fourteen years of age to play parts in their productions. Films are shot all over Europe. We also look for good models from the USA as we will pay travel expenses, etc. Beautiful girls can make much, much money."[24]

"Collector is looking for unusual photos of children and animals. Highest prices paid. 100 percent discretion."[25]

"Will give away child pornography collection for 'share in the fun' of anyone having daughter ten to fifteen years old. I want to pass on my large collection to somebody younger instead of it being found after my death by someone not understanding my inclinations or passions."[26]

"Couple, thirty-three/thirty-four, daughter thirteen. She has been busy with sex with us nearly from her birth on and we all still love it."[27]

A hotel owner offers free vacations to girls between six and eleven years old.[28]

"Very rich young man will pay any price you ask for sex

with lovely girl any age under twelve." (This last advertisement, and some aforementioned, raises the question of whether these classifieds promote child abduction for financial gain.)[29]

(4) A Resource for Arguments Justifying Child Sex

Though hardly convincing, the pedophile has a host of arguments "justifying" his sexual perversion.

A former Member of the Upper House of the Dutch Parliament, Edward Brongersma, wrote in *Lolita* that children want sex with adults and when refused they view themselves as "rejected sexual being(s)."

In language befitting a politician, Brongersma wrote, "The result is the abandonment to an emotionally impoverished but materially highly demanding society, whose members wish to annihilate the flesh by an exaggerated hygiene and the use of deodorant spray and soap."

Saying the "judge must be just," he concluded that "it is not just to throw a citizen in jail for behaviour that is born of a positive inclination and is possibly valued."[30]

The editors of *Lolita* magazine write, "If children wanted their sex with other children, okay. If they choose to have it with a sympathetic adult, also okay. Sex is one of the most important things in life and it can only be good when it is learned in a loving way with knowing partners. It is madness to say that love for children always has to be without sexual feelings. In most of the cases the sexual longings are felt by both the adult and the child and it is only natural when they express these feelings and so learn the value of loving sexual satisfaction. . . . In the fifty magazines which have been put out now by *Lolita*, (we have) tried to give the lovely girl back her sexuality, it is rightfully hers."[31]

The editors of *Nudist Moppets* take a more detailed approach to justifying child sex.

In an article titled, "To be Young, Free *and* Admired," the editors reason: "Since all human beings are born into this world

totally nude, it can be safely assumed that the state of naked-
ness is fundamental." Only through parental teaching do children learn certain parts of the body are "indecent" and must be
concealed. This is evident by children who "are least concerned
about the relative morality of degree of clothing. Left to their
own devices, children would only dress for fun, style or comfort." Unless, of course, they are "indoctrinated."

The editors move on to mock parents who teach girls
decent dress, modesty, and acts. "And so it goes on, absurdity
after absurdity. The result is that so-called 'modesty' often
becomes an obsession." Such "brainwashing" results in "ner-
vous habits such as constantly tugging at the hem of her skirt
and the legs of her shorts . . . anything to avoid the horrible
consequences of being attacked and ravished." A boy's smile
brings "fear" rather than "happiness."

"Little girls often grow up with a basic distrust of men.

"Young girls indeed *are* attractive to men. It is completely
natural for men to want to look at them." (Interestingly, photos
of three- to four-year-old girls accompany this article.) "Girls
who are on their way to full physical maturity have a special
charm and attraction all their own. . . . A happy smile and a 'hi'
from such a girl can make a dull day bright. Yes, men do look
at young girls."

Clothes "are barriers to communications because they
produce involuntary judgments of relative social class and
wealth. Persons who lack self-confidence hide behind clothes.
. . . Without the latest flashy fashions and undergarment engi-
neering wonders, [a woman has] to rely on her own personality."

But, for some, all these constraints are being cast aside.
"Best of all, other lucky youngsters—with their parents' encouragement and participation—are growing up with nudism.
. . . These families have cut through the taboos. They have
developed a healthier, more sensible perspective, free from the
hangups of a sheltered, shrouded life. They know what it
means to be happy and free."[32]

(5) A Visual Device to Manipulate Children

For the most part, children are taught to trust adults and to trust books, magazines, and newspapers. The child, therefore, is an easy victim for the adult pedophile who uses child pornography to demonstrate the "fun" of having sex with adults.

Relying on the child's natural curiosity about sex, the pedophile first uses child pornography as a psychological aid by showing his victim that other adults have sex with children and that the children are enjoying themselves. Then, after establishing sex with adults as both normal and pleasurable, the pedophile uses child pornography as an instructional aid by showing the child how the actual sex acts are performed.

Having lowered the child's inhibitions and aroused his curiosity, the pedophile is now in a position to convince the victim to perform similar poses and activities.

Personal Child Pornography Items

Because the child victim soon grows out of desired age, most pedophiles find it important to keep mementos of the sexual acts for future recall and gratification. Photos, diaries, motion pictures, and even pubic hair, soiled underwear, and objects used to violate the children are often stored away so the pedophile can recreate the sexual experience later. (When writing the diary, however, it is not unusual for the pedophile to distort the experience and hold the child responsible for the sexual overtures and acts rather than himself.) Frequently, the pedophile simply mimics the stories, photographs, and abuses he has observed in child pornography films and magazines.

Sex Rings

If the pedophile does not share or communicate his sexual molestings with others, he is known as operating a "solo sex ring" by law enforcement officials. But when he begins to trade photos, letters, audio tapes, and children with other pedophiles, he is known as operating a "transition sex ring." And when the pedophile joins other pedophiles in a well-structured organization, recruiting children, producing pornography, and delivering sexual services to an extensive network of customers, he is known as operating a "syndicated sex ring."

Two examples of "syndicated sex rings" include the following:

• West Hollywood, California. Hundreds of naive young boys from Mexico and Canada thought they were going to make it big in Hollywood—appearing in motion pictures, commercials, and modeling—when they were recruited to pose nude for *Male Image*. But when the photographs were developed, they were published in homosexual publications—without the child's consent or knowledge. Allan L., forty-six, and Michael L., thirty-six, who operated the "modeling agency," then used the published pictures to bribe, intimidate, and exploit the boys into participating in an international prostitution and pornography ring. The scam was brought to the attention of the Los Angeles Police Department when Michael L. brought several hundred negatives of nude boys to a Fotomat store in Bellingham, Washington. After an eleven-month investigation, police raided Michael L.'s home in Vancouver and found an inch-thick "chicken book" listing "customers, acts of sex, and amounts paid."[33]

• San Jose, California. Recruiting high school girls to join this syndicated sex ring was no more difficult than placing an advertisement for household chores on store bulletin boards. At first Walter H., fifty-eight, offered the girls money for cleaning his apartment, then for posing in photographs, then for sexual favors, then for posing while performing sexual acts. These girls would then bring their male and female friends into the sex ring where they were paid twenty to fifty dollars to pose in still and motion pictures committing sex acts with adults and other minors. But Walter H. did not operate alone. He worked closely with Earl M., sixty, who sold the pictures to customers on a computerized mailing list that ran into the hundreds. When police apprehended Earl M. they found carefully coded filing cabinets with photographs of every type of sexual perversion—straight child pornography, bestiality, bondage, domination, sado-masochism, and human degradation. The customers would write letters to Earl M. requesting specific activities. If none were available, Earl M. would enlist the services of Walter H. who would pay the children to perform those acts. The children, for their part, were motivated by nothing more than money, liquor, marijuana, attention, and emotional support. The scam was uncovered by San Jose police after a fifteen-year-old girl left a letter to her mother on the living room table describing her sexual encounters with Walter H.[34]

Day-Care Sex Rings

An even more sinister syndicated sex ring (more sinister because parents unwittingly drop their children off at the doorsteps of the child molesters) are day-care centers that are formed for the sole purpose of sexually exploiting children.

Around the country police have arrested a number of day-care center operators who have either confessed to raping and molesting children or police have found such positive signs of abuse as gonorrhea of the throat, vaginal and rectal penetration and diseases, or photographs.

Said one leading expert, Kee MacFarlane, "The proposition that a totally unknown number of preschools and other child care institutions could be serving such purposes is formidable, but many of the cases currently under investigation . . . could only have existed under these conspiratorial circumstances."

MacFarlane, who is the director of Child Sexual Abuse Diagnostic Center of the Children's Institute International in Los Angeles, has provided medical and psychological evaluation for more than four hundred children who claim to have been sexually abused by personnel in almost a dozen preschools.

According to her findings, children between two and five

years old are forced into every conceivable sex act with adults, other children, and both sexes. The children are tricked through games, rewards of treats and candy, and the influence of drugs. Some children are "pornographically photographed with such frequency that they view it as part of their daily routine." Often the children are taken from the schools and handed over to strangers. To silence the children, operators of the school subject the children to "bizarre rituals involving violence, animals, scatological behavior and what they perceive as magic." Some have been threatened with weapons, or harm to their families, or have been intimidated by being forced to observe the slaughter of animals.

"If this thing sounds unimaginable to you, you are not alone. All of us involved with these cases struggle with the same thing," MacFarlane told a congressional committee.

MacFarlane conceded that some child care facilities have only one individual who, unbeknownst to other staff members, uses his or her position as an access for sexual gratification.

But when the facility has "multiple suspected perpetrators" who work with a large ring of adults outside the school, then what "we find ourselves dealing with is no less than a conspiracy—an organized operation of child predators designed to prevent detection. . . . The preschool, in such a case, serves as a ruse for a larger, unthinkable network of crimes against children."[35]

Child Abductions

But more disturbing than "neighborhood pedophiles" and "syndicated sex rings" are child molesters who abduct children—for a lifetime.

Between six thousand and fifty thousand children are abducted each year. Only a few of these are ever recovered alive. Reasons vary for the abductions. Some are stolen by childless couples or by an abductor to sell to a childless couple. Some are kidnapped for such deviant reasons as ransom or, in one case, to have a strong lad around the house. Many are abducted by sadistic killers. Most are abducted by non-custodial parents. Still others are abducted by pedophiles who sexually abuse the child until he grows to puberty.

The abduction is generally friendly, without force, without trails, and without leads.

"Kids are trusting people," explained FBI assistant director in charge, Lee Laster. "And when it comes to luring children off the street, a lot of things work. The abductors use pets, puppies, candy, or just being nice. They lie to them. Tell them it's being done for their parents. They might even use a uniform. There have been instances where people have indicated they were a police officer and used a uniform. Why? Because kids are trusting."[36]

"In many instances," he said, "they might be kidnapped right off the street. In some instances he may be enticed away from his home life because what the pedophile offers is better than what the child has at home."

Apparently, no place is totally safe from the child abductor. Children have been stolen from stores, on their way to and from school, from parks, while working paper routes, from front yards—even from their parent's arms.

To find out whether children are being abducted for sexual purposes, Mr. Laster approved the formation of an FBI task force to determine whether missing children are being used in child pornography, prostitution, and other sexually exploitive situations.

Reliable statistics do not exist, but it appears that one of three things is likely to happen to a child abducted for sexual purposes: (1) The child is purposely killed for sadistic reasons or to prevent disclosure. (2) The child is accidentally killed by the sexual act. (Many die from rectal hemorrhage.) (3) The child becomes the sexual slave of the abductor and may even be marketed to others for prostitution and pornography. In this last case, the child is generally discarded upon reaching puberty whereupon most become street urchins.

Most children stay with their captors due to loyalty, embarrassment, or not knowing they have a home to go to. During their stay they are subjected to every sort of sexual abuse and many become addicted to drugs and alcohol, which further complicates the enormous psychological pressures they already suffer.

"You get into some wild, wild things here and you wonder how mankind can involve themselves with it. . . . Is the child going to think this is a normal thing that happens to kids? Can you imagine the thinking of a child at this point? I really can't. I have trouble deciding in my own mind how the kids are going to look at adults in general," said Mr. Laster whose position is second only to FBI Director William Webster.

Gary Hewitt, executive director for the Center for Missing Children in Rochester, New York, said abducted children go through three stages when adjusting to their new environment. "First they go through a psychological mourning process. They protest. 'I want to go home.' They cry. Then they go through a period of despair. They become listless, withdrawn. Finally, they adapt to their caretaker. They do it quickly—within a few days—because they need to. And that becomes the most important person besides his family members in their life."[37]

Passing Around the Abducted Child

Mr. Laster added that though pedophiles do not represent a structured organization, they are able to communicate effectively with one another and, as a result, do represent "a loose coalition in the manner of a national organization."

He said, "We are finding that there is some sort of ability on the part of the people on the West Coast to talk to people on the East Coast. And we have had instances where kids have been carried or transported from one state to another or from one coast to another for pornography and prostitution purposes."

"Kids *are* being passed around," he said. "The child pornography filmmaker in Queens knows a guy in Chicago doing the same thing, or in Los Angeles doing the same thing. In fact, there may be instances where there's a child here that's done good in a film and they ship the child somewhere else to make a film out there."

Mr. Laster, whose FBI office is located in New York City, said, "In state hearings here there was testimony that some pimps are shuttling young kids from one city to another. They can make a boy available for a party, for a weekend, or a week, or a permanent basis if they want it.

"We're finding a great deal of organization. Do you want a film, picture, or prostitute? If you know the right phone number that's not a great problem. We hope that within a year or two it will be a much greater problem. It's our very earnest wish that we can have a tremendous impact on this problem."

The Short-Term Abduction

Gary Hewitt, whose Center for Missing Children organization provides therapy and counseling to families when children return from an abduction, said child molesters are more likely to abduct children for short periods of time rather than a lifetime.

"That's happening all the time. Kids are abducted and sexually abused for an hour, two hours, four hours—even a few days—and then dropped off in cases that never get reported."

Mr. Hewitt said, "Since most people who abduct children aren't being caught, we're getting most of our information from the kids. Therefore we don't know the history of the abduction, such as whether the abductor was deeply involved in child pornography before kidnapping kids. But as an example of a short-term abduction, I just worked on a case here in Rochester and a youngster, who was preoccupied, said, 'I didn't tell my mom and dad this summer I had sex with a man for two hours. My bathing suit was taken off and these people did this and that to me.' His parents had complained that the boy had been experiencing difficulty concentrating. Well, that's why. These people said we'll hurt you, we'll kill you if you tell anybody."

Mr. Hewitt agreed with the FBI that children abducted for longer periods are generally discarded upon reaching puberty, after which they move onto the streets.

"People in the underground say kids are out on the street, afraid to go home—no longer abducted—who have moved into an anti-social environment such as prostitution."

Child Prostitution

Child prostitution actually serves as a deterrent to abduction in some major cities.

Said Mr. Hewitt, "In New York City child prostitution is so high, in fact, if somebody wanted to have sex with a child, all they need do is go down to the arcades in Times Square, pick up their kid, have sex, photograph them, or whatever, and let the kid go. Pay them some money and they don't have to abduct the child."

The FBI estimates that more than six hundred thousand child prostitutes are roaming the nation's streets.[38]

Sergeant Samuel Alberti, who heads the pedophilia unit of the Manhattan South Public Morals Division, admitted that New York City does suffer a problem with child prostitution by children as young as eight years old.[39]

"We do have areas in the city of New York where you have young children—I call them children because they are—who come from very deprived, very poor homes. Most of them are black or Hispanic who, for some reason or another, prostitute themselves out of need for love and affection and money," he said.

Sergeant Alberti was reluctant to call these children "prostitutes," however.

"Prostitution is really for gain. It's unemotional, and it's done in a business-like manner," he said. "And by far these children are not doing this in a removed, business-like manner. That's my interpretation. And I find that these pedas (pedophiles) know that these children are in a desperate situation. And they entice them with money, clothing, food, a decent environment of comfort, love—which they don't get at home."

So, unlike women prostitutes who sell their bodies for profit, children sell their bodies for attention, food, a home to go to at night, and a feeling of love from another human being.

"It's a sad commentary, but the fact is you start trying to—what would you say—role play. What would you do if you were in their spot, and you don't have a family, or a family doesn't care about you, or kicks you out on the street, or maybe your mother's a pros (prostitute) and your father's a junkie or whatever the case may be. And you say, 'What's better: Being with these pedas or being out on the streets?' You're really torn by these certain situations," Sergeant Alberti said.

Picking Up the Child Prostitute

Agreeing that Times Square is an ideal location for picking up child prostitutes, Sergeant Alberti said pedophiles come from any of New York City's five adjoining boroughs and its neighboring states, New Jersey and Connecticut. Some will even move to the city for closer accessibility.

If the pedophile is unsure where to find children, he can contact a "steerer"—a person acting as a third party who directs a pedophile to where child prostitutes can be found.

Explaining how the pedophile picks up a child prostitute, Sergeant Alberti said, "He will go down to Times Square and see a boy. He'll say to the boy, 'How are you doing, can I help you, you seem to be lonely.' Or he might talk to him and say, 'I want to be your friend. Can I buy you something? Are you hungry?' He might take him to a restaurant, or walk to McDonald's, or whatever it is. And he might say, 'Do you want to play some video games?' And this might go on a couple of times. Then he says, 'Do you want to come up to my house?'

"And we find that many times they use drugs on these children. What they'll do is say, 'Do you want to smoke a little marijuana or take some pills?' And he might get them drunk. And he'll start to massage the boy, playing with his privates, and so on. And if the boy backs off, he'll just disregard it.

"There might be another time and he'll have video games at his home, or some sort of visual entertainment. It could be child pornography. Or it could be adult pornography—anything to stimulate the boy. And he'll just keep progressing until he can get the child into a situation where he can manipulate the boy.

"I know their appetite runs three or four kids a night," Sergeant Alberti said.

Some of the boys manage to "turn the tables" on the pedophile—especially if the pedophile is a respected community member.

"Some children wait outside arcades to be picked up," Sergeant Alberti said. "They are aware that if they do eventually get involved with these men they have them over a barrel—because most of these pedophiles have prominent jobs. Alright, the doctor and the lawyer, he's not going to go down to Times Square, but he's going to get another pedophile to bring the boy home."

Continuing, he said, "The fact of the matter is, these boys then turn the tables on these men—because they are constantly being told, 'Don't tell anybody, don't tell anybody.' We had a case here where this doctor had a thirteen-year-old boy. And the boy's telling this doctor, calling him by his first name, I want this, and I want that. Because they know they've got them over a barrel. So it can be a two-way street."

Midway through this interview the telephone rings and Sergeant Alberti goes to a private room to answer the call. Fifteen minutes later he returns and, noticeably agitated, said, "This is what we're talking about here.

"We've got a fifteen-year-old male Hispanic who was down the Times Square area who was picked up by a male black. He was going to be a 'trick,' in other words he was going to pay the kid twenty-five, thirty-five dollars, whatever. And he brought him up to 116th, 115th Street to a hotel. And he gave the boy some drugs, so on and so forth. And he got the boy to sodomize him. Now the boy wants to leave. But the man refused to let him leave. He locked the door, took his clothes. Now he's forcing the boy to perform sex on him and he's continuing to sodomize the boy. Well, here's the typical situation."

The typical situation? What an alarming statement.

Recovering from Sexual Abuse

The effects of sexual abuse on children are varied.

Many children experience flashbacks, nightmares, hyper-alertness, bed-wetting, aggressiveness, and insomnia. Some suffer from intrusive thoughts and gender identity conflicts. One child developed a hundred separate personalities. Bodily damage includes torn vaginas and rectums and venereal diseases. Some complain of continual stomachaches, headaches, and lack of appetite. Others become distressed when strangers enter the home. And the abused child may refuse to go to church or school. Some even become sexually aggressive toward their peers and perform the same acts on them. And abused children may use sex to acquire recognition, attention, or validation. Still others, as mentioned, become addicted to drugs or alcohol or resort to prostitution.

But at least 25 percent of molested children master their anxieties of abuse.[40]

The emotional effects on parents can be equally as severe.

Said Gary Hewitt, "Parents have more difficulty than the kids most times. You know, 'Is my child going to be messed up for life?' And that's not true at all. Kids who are sexually abused can get over it."

Getting Off the Hook

The pedophile tries a number of strategies to absolve himself of the crime.

According to Kenneth V. Lanning, an FBI agent, and Ann W. Burgess, a professor of psychiatric nursing, the pedophile's first reaction is complete denial. He may act shocked, surprised, or even indignant about the allegation. He claims he knows nothing.

Neighbors, friends, relatives—all may come to his support and insist he is a wonderful person. They may even be uncooperative and hinder the investigation.

If evidence is convincing, he'll minimize both quantity and quality. "If a certain act was performed a hundred times, the victim might claim it happened only thirty times, and the offenders might claim it happened only twice," the experts wrote in the FBI's Law Enforcement Bulletin.

The pedophile will then attempt to justify his acts. He'll say he cares more for the child than his parents, that his relationship with the child has actually been beneficial. He may claim he has been under stress, or suffers a drinking problem, or that he didn't know the victim's age. He may even blame the victim and claim that it was he—the pedophile—who had to control himself. Pedophile manuals even advocate this tactic when all else fails. It is interesting to note that few pedophiles admit this sickness until they are arrested or until other tactics fail.

The pedophile may also play the "sympathy game." He'll try to get people to feel sorry for him. He'll say he's sorry and present evidence that he's a nice guy—a pillar of the community, a devoted family man, a military vet, a church leader, a "victim of circumstances with many personal problems."

The "sympathy game" with the "sick game" is a "very effective tactic for the pedophile to use to escape responsibility for his behavior," the authors say.

Some will go on the offensive, such as raise the issue of gay rights. And some may plead guilty by reason of insanity.[41]

Child Sex Tours

Very little is known about pedophilia on an international scale. But what little is known is quite disturbing.

In a 1982 study, Katie David, of the Defence for Children International (DCI) in Geneva, found evidence of child sex package tours being offered in the Netherlands, West Germany, Japan, and the United States.

The tours took people to Sri Lanka, Thailand, and the Philippines. Once there, tourist guides help negotiate prices, offer advice on which hotels to use, explain how to circumvent local laws and deal effectively with local officials, and a host of other benefits. A leading magazine in this field, Ms. David found, is called *Sparticus*. But she noted that there were other magazines offering child sex tours and even child sex tourist agencies.

Two hundred thousand young male prostitutes are reportedly available in Bangkok, Thailand, and two thousand child prostitutes have been reported in Colombo, Sri Lanka. In Phuket, Thailand, thirteen-year-old girls are said to be paid two dollars a week, drugged, beaten, and tied to beds in brothels to the amusement of tourists. And there were reports in September 1984 of child auctions in Amsterdam, which is believed not to be an isolated event, but rather an example of activity that takes place in a variety of nations—including this one.[42]

Pedophilia in Action

Having examined the activities and nature of the pedophile, the reader now has a better understanding of the child molester. But this is not enough; it's too static, too enigmatic. Like pieces of a broken puzzle, the reader only has broken images of his child's enemy. Those pieces must now be put together. The reader must be able to visualize the child molester in action. We know his seductive tactics—child pornography, money, affection, a fatherly image, etc. And we know his hiding places— video arcades, youth groups, public swimming pools, etc. But we have yet to see the molester in action—how he ruthlessly manipulates the mind and soul of each child he rapes. In the following three chapters, the reader will examine the operations of three convicted child molesters. When finished, the pieces of the puzzle will come together and the reader will finally gain a visual understanding of the pedophile—an understanding of great importance if parents hope to protect their children from the preying hands of the child molester.

FOUR

THE TEN-YEAR HANGOVER

Robert V. did not remember a thing about the previous night. But seven-year-old Susan painfully reminded him.

Said the forty-two-year-old retired sailor, "I was baby-sitting the girl—her mother worked all night long—and I was drinking pretty heavily. I forgot what I did to her, but she told me about it—how I had sex with her. She seemed quite enthused. But it wasn't exactly the type of thing I wanted to wake up to."

Recently divorced after fifteen years of marriage, a patron of adult movies and strip joints, a heavy drinker, unable to find a girlfriend, emotionally unstable, no one to talk to, and then asked to baby-sit young girls all night long—Robert V. was a recipe for disaster.

Father of two teenagers, Robert V. said he was deeply moved and shocked by his divorce. "I ate, ate, and ate. And I drank. And I drank some more. My job performance—I was working as a maintenance man at an apartment complex—my job performance went steadily downhill. I wanted to talk to somebody, but I didn't know who. I tried going with another girl, but she was checking up on me after two months—you know, she wanted to know what was I doing, who was I going out with, stuff like that. It was like being married all over again. So this was not going too well, so I broke up with her."

Speaking constantly with his hands, Robert V. looked much older than his age. His hair receded and was greased back. Heavy wrinkles accentuated his tired brown eyes. And his triangular face bore the marks of a man under great stress.

He smoked repeatedly, looked directly into the eyes, and spoke out of the side of his mouth. He was pleasant, thin, medium height, and always speaking with a smile. He had a noticeable habit of licking his lips as he talked and a disturbing habit of speaking through his nostrils.

He capsulized his life after divorce: "It started off like a snowball at the top of a hill which, as it rolled, it got bigger and bigger and bigger until it finally burst at the bottom."

Susan . . . and Friends

Robert V. did not know whether to believe Susan when she told him that they had had sex the night before. "But it happened again—and that time I remembered. Inwardly I know this is not right, this is wrong. But I didn't know what to do about it," he said, recalling the shame.

Susan quickly added to Robert V.'s miseries by bringing another seven-year-old girl, Nancy, to his apartment. "Now they both want sex," he said. "I had previously baby-sat this second girl too, but I never touched her, and I didn't want to touch her now. Well, the first couple of times I made excuses. But they were very persistent. Then the first girl, Susan, threatened to tell her mother unless I agreed to have sex with them. Out of fear I went ahead. Maybe, I thought, this would keep them quiet, maybe this would end it."

But it didn't.

"Bright and early every Saturday morning one or both girls would be at the door. They wanted to get involved. Sometimes I wouldn't open the door. Sometimes I made excuses. But I didn't want to get this first girl mad because she would tell. So I would get half drunk and do what they wanted me to do."

He absolved himself by saying, "I have no sexual inclinations for young girls. And I never enjoyed any of the encounters. Basically, I was just satisfying their desires.

"The children wanted somebody to talk to. Their mothers didn't know where their daughters were. But they knew where I was. If their bicycles needed fixing, they knew I would fix it," he said.

Afraid of getting caught, Robert V. was consumed with paranoia. "Every time a police car drove into the apartment complex my heart would jump fifty beats. And if I didn't know where the police car went, I would get in my truck and go look for it."

After the school year ended, Nancy—the second girl—went south to stay with a relative. Robert V. breathed a sigh of relief; he expected things to improve. It was doubtful, he thought, that Susan would come over to the house by herself. And he was right. She didn't. She brought another friend: Mary, age eight.

"Both of these girls went into the bathroom—they said they had to go. But what they did was take off their clothes and go into the bedroom. Well, I started balking."

But because his drinking problem was not under control, Robert V. did not balk for long. "Basically, I had oral sex on them, or I fondled them. The third girl, the most willing, wanted intercourse, but I said she was too young. I think they got the idea from adult pornography.

"They usually showed up together and I accommodated them—knowing full well that I was getting deeper and deeper involved. It became a ritual."

Trying to Escape

In an attempt to stop the rendezvous, he resorted to old, worn-out—and ineffective—strategies—hiding in his truck, waiting at the bar until it was safe to go home, pretending he was leaving when they visited.

Robert V. thought about professional help. But only briefly, long enough to get the names and addresses of psychologists out of the Yellow Pages. "I was afraid to go to them. I knew that whoever I sought help from would turn me in.

"The real icing on the cake came during the first part of August (1982)," he said. "The first and third girl came over and this third girl brought her older brother. Well, I was working on their bikes and I offered them some cokes. It was a hot day. They went into my apartment and the girls went into the bathroom and stripped naked! In front of the one girl's brother! Well, now I know I'm going to get caught. Fortunately the phone rang and I pretended I had to go somewhere. Nothing happened, but I knew I had to finally put an end to these episodes."

When he met the girls later, he said, "I sat the first girl down and I told her this thing isn't right, that somebody was going to find out if it continued. I told her it had to stop.

"Evidently, she began to feel the same way because after that there were only two episodes the whole month, where before there were three encounters a week," he said. The third girl started backing off too. By late August there were no more incidents.

Nevertheless, Robert V. was obsessed with fear of being caught. Would the children talk? Would their actions tip somebody off? His freedom rested in the hands of three small children and their willingness to keep a secret. "The only way I could sleep was to drink until I was drunk. I burned many a cigarette on my chest."

But things went smoothly for Robert V. He moved to an apartment across the main entrance—an entrance the children were forbidden to cross because it was busy with traffic. He ate Thanksgiving dinner with one of the mothers of the three abused children. He even took the mother out on a date! And further flirting with disaster, he baby-sat two of the children on several occasions. "But I made d--- sure nothing happened. I even curbed my drinking to make sure," he said.

"I was happy the sex encounters were over. But I still had fear, an inner disgust, a dread of getting caught. Deep down inside I knew I was going to get caught. But outwardly I was hoping it would all blow over."

An Unexpected, Unwanted Gift

Early Monday morning before Christmas, Robert V. stumbled into his apartment—drunk as usual—but sober enough to notice a business card and a search warrant on the living room end table. Susan had finally turned him in to the police. He searched the apartment to see what, if anything, the police had taken. Missing were some adult magazines, an 8mm movie camera, and a Kodak instant camera.

"I immediately got sober," he said. "Nine million thoughts ran through my head. And the biggest one staring me in the face was, 'Well, the cat's out of the bag, what are you going to do?' "

He had all sorts of choices. "I could run," he thought as he popped open a can of beer. He read the warrant again . . . and again. "If I run I was proving myself guilty. And I would have to run forever, or until I got caught. And what would happen to my kids? I would never see them again if I ran."

He called his boss at 7:00 A.M. "I told him I wouldn't be working today. But I knew I wouldn't be working again for a long time. I had made my decision. I knew I was wrong when the thing started. I made my bed, I might as well go lie in it."

He took a shower. The choices continued to haunt him. Run. Plead not guilty. Accuse the children of lying. Lie in the bed he made for himself.

He dressed, got in the car, and "made the last drive I was going to have for quite a while. I had made another decision: Tell the truth. I didn't want to drag these kids into court; they had been through enough already."

In June 1983, Robert V. was convicted of forcible sodomy,

taking indecent liberties, and aggravated sexual battery. He was sentenced to ten years in prison and ten years supervised probation.

"I finally broke down. I bawled my head off. I lost my wife, my kids, and now I'm off to jail. I went many nights without sleep. And when I did sleep I had nightmares. I kept seeing it all over again. And if children came on TV, I felt like hiding myself. I thought I was worse than somebody who took somebody's life. Only a child murderer could be worse.

"But I was glad it was over," he said. "It took a lot of anxiety out of me—fear and grief. . . . My life was in the gutter. You can't feel proud about yourself. It's something you want to bury, but you can't. So I was glad I turned myself in."

Finding Forgiveness

"It took me a while to believe God could forgive me of my sins," he said. "In prison I picked up a piece of literature. I don't remember what it said, but it spoke about the Bible. I then went to speak with the chaplain. He didn't condone what I did, but he didn't condemn me either. He gave me a little bit of hope. A little bit of insight into myself. And I appreciated his honesty."

Robert V. explained that he didn't turn to God in the beginning because he was "a little irked at religion."

"Religion was what ruined my marriage," he said.

He explained, "My wife was deeply involved in religion. And so was I, but not as deep. I used to be an usher and a layman in the armed forces chapel. But my wife wanted more. She wanted to be a pastor. So she entered a seminary in Louisville, Kentucky. She got so religious she forgot her marriage vows. Now I don't know what she's doing."

But life without religion hardly improved his lot. "I couldn't find help with close friends, so I said, 'Forget it, I'm going to try to handle this thing myself.' But now I know, sometimes Jesus Christ will help you," he said, innocently enough.

"In prison I read the *Good News Bible* cover to cover in thirty days. Then I read the *King James Version*. And I still read it, though not every day. But I do read it when I'm troubled or upset."

Cutting off all ties with the past, Robert V. gave away all his belongings—military awards, furniture, clothing, even his 1964 Mustang. When he gets out, he said, he'll start anew.

"I'll get myself right back and I'll make myself a name again—a good name."

GIVE AN INCH, TAKE A MILE

Sitting in a holding room at a maximum security prison, Ricky Lee G. was motionless—his eyes were plastered against the wall straight ahead, his hands were trapped by the pockets of his blue denim jacket, and his feet were glued to a tile on the floor. Ricky Lee G., though only twenty-seven years old, was like a dead man losing the battle against rigor mortis. Sentenced to seventy years in prison for molesting seven boys and two girls, perhaps the young man's life was over, perhaps the King of Death had a right to cast its shadow on another victim.

Ever since he was eight years old, Ricky Lee was sexually attracted to boys.

"I found pleasure in rubbing up against other boys in school lunch lines," he said. Soon he was having "encounters" with cousins and neighborhood kids. "We'd play doctor and I would give them an exam," he explained the strategy. "As I grew, I took more and more liberties."

By age fourteen, Ricky discovered that older men were willing to pay for young boy prostitutes.

"I would hustle at an old Greyhound Bus terminal for twenty dollars—enough to buy an ounce of reefer. There were maybe fifteen to twenty of us. We would approach any car that slowed down. The men were in their thirties, forties, and fifties—mostly businessmen. I was arrested three times, but I never went to court, never paid any fines, and never went to jail. The judge called the arrests entrapments."

Early Warning Signs
Ricky Lee escaped jail, but he did not escape psychosis.

As early as fourth grade, Ricky's teachers were complaining of his mental problems. By ninth grade his mental instability forced him to quit school.

According to Ricky's account, his principal "harassed him" and asked him to leave school because of his unusual religious behavior.

"I was raised in a Christian family," he said. "But for some reason my family stopped going to church. When I was fourteen I decided to go back to church. But I quickly became known as a religious eccentric to school officials and classmates. Shortly afterwards I withdrew from school because the principal asked me to leave—he didn't like my meditation or carrying a huge Bible.

"At the time I was a religious person. I can say now I wasn't a Christian. I thought I was. But if I was I wouldn't have been carrying on a homosexual relationship. Anyway, I quit going to church soon afterwards."

According to the principal's account, Ricky Lee became heavily involved in religion, going into trances, speaking in tongues, and disrupting other students. The principal sent him home twice but denies asking Ricky to withdraw from school. At the time his academic performance was poor, mostly Ds. He was reading at a fifth grade level. And his IQ was a dismal eighty-two—a level reserved for morons.

Ricky's former guidance counselor referred to him as "weird" with "no personal pride." An elementary teacher remembered him as a "shy, quiet loner" lacking any self-esteem, "hypersensitive to criticism," with frequent outbursts of temper.

Perhaps much of Ricky's pressure to quit school came from other students. At fourteen he became "known as a faggot," which destroyed whatever rapport he had with his classmates.

No Help to Be Found

Ricky never abandoned his desire for young boys, even though his sexual acts with youths were exacting a great mental toll.

As Ricky Lee explained, "I knew homosexuality was wrong when I was thirteen. Well, if homosexuality is wrong, certainly committing sex acts with small boys is wrong."

Ricky tried, in a roundabout way, to turn himself in. He went to police and medical authorities and told them he was a homosexual. He had hoped that by being medically treated for his homosexuality he would also be rid of his pedophilia. But the police told him homosexuality was not against the law, and the medical profession told him homosexuality was an alternative lifestyle.

"The courts left the door wide open," he said. "The court says consensual sex is okay. The court said going against nature is okay. Well, if you give somebody an inch they're going to take a mile."

And Ricky Lee took that mile, and more!

How many children did Ricky Lee molest? Fifty? Seventy-five? A hundred? With each new figure, Ricky shook his head and shrugged his shoulders.

More than a hundred?

"I don't know how many," he complained. "Between 125 and 150 kids, I suppose." That admission was painful. He quickly and shamefully turned his head away and said, "It's sick. It's sick."

Sick? Yes. But how was it possible? How was it possible

for one pedophile to find more than 125 young boys available for sexual abuse in a small town?

Like Opening a Refrigerator Door

"You find them just about anyplace: amusements, swimming pools, Lakeside (an amusement park), Happy's Flea Market and skating rink, video arcades, pool halls, shopping centers, and any shopping mall. It's easy to find boys nine years old on up by themselves. Oftentimes they start the conversation. Kids know. Believe you me, they can tell a homosexual a mile off. . . . It's as natural as going to the refrigerator door and getting food out. A lot of times I didn't need to say anything at all, we'd just go for a walk."

It's hard to accept these statements—that little boys know how to prostitute themselves, that they are as vulnerable as cold meat and a jar of mayonnaise, that they would so readily take a walk to the woods, an alley, or a public bathroom.

Ricky Lee befriended many of these boys. "We were friends. I was like a big brother to them. I would handle their problems, give them money. They knew that anytime they needed something they could come to me."

But Ricky Lee's friendship with the young lads smacked more of a tactical move to acquire more children than a genuine friendship. "The boys would bring their friends, their brothers over—every time for sex." He would frequently use beer, bourbon, money, and gifts to lower their inhibitions.

Ricky said he learned much of his tactical moves by reading pedophile "trash books" that are sold illegally in video peep shops. "The books cost me anywhere from two to fifty dollars. They weren't hard to get because I was friends with the bookstore owners. Some books were sold right out on the shelves. If the detectives in the city would do their jobs the cover of the book would tell them what's inside. But they're not doing their jobs.

"I read such paperback books as *Bang the Boy, Bang the Teacher,* and *Hard Teacher*—all of which are supposed to be novels. Even so, they teach the pedophile quite a lot. They told you exactly what to do and how to go about it. How to hold a conversation with a child, and how to talk to a child without the boy thinking there is anything wrong with the sex."

"They Don't Care"

On several occasions, the boys—all minors—became Ricky Lee's "live-in boyfriends." One such child was a fourteen-year-old boy named Bruce.

Ricky explained, "Bruce was a young boy who lived with me after his mom threw him out of the house for stealing a roll of fifty pennies. He was hanging out one night at a Hopin store (a convenience food market), and I introduced myself to him. When I heard that he had been thrown out of his home, I said he could live with me. I said he could sleep in the bedroom, that I would sleep on the couch. And when he first moved in that's the way we lived.

"Well, after he had been living with me a while he got caught stealing. At his trial, his mom said she wanted him out of her hair, that she didn't care what the court did with him. The boy told the judge that he was staying with me. Well, the judge knew who I was, that I was a homosexual. I had been before him on sex charges before. Even so, the judge didn't want to keep the boy locked up, so he placed Bruce in my custody.

"Well, that was another thing that told me, 'They don't care!' They're letting the boy stay with me, even though they know I'm a homosexual! They're letting me sign his release papers!"

The court decision was an open invitation for Ricky Lee to act on his homosexual attraction to the boy. Of course he was going to interpret it as a validation of his sexual activities. Ricky Lee knew his pedophilia acts were wrong. Yet society, without so much as a blush, was not only willing to accept his sins against nature—homosexuality—but was willing to place a runaway child within his custody.

A Foster Parent Fostering Insanity

The absurdity of the court's decision does not end here. Had the judge investigated Ricky Lee's medical background, the court would have learned that Ricky Lee was an abuser of alcohol and drugs, that he had attempted suicide, that he had admitted to having sexual problems with children, and that between July 1976 and September 1983 he had been hospitalized for mental reasons no fewer than twenty-seven times!

Medical records indicate that Ricky Lee was a habitual and excessive drinker until 1979. And even though he eventually gained control over his alcoholism, he never curtailed his marijuana use. Since age sixteen, Ricky Lee smoked marijuana two to three times a day. He experimented with LSD and amphetamines. During his late teens he sniffed glue, gasoline, and aerosol deodorants—and he did it often. He knew it could give him brain damage, but he said he didn't care.

Feeling he had "nothing to live for," Ricky Lee continually threatened to "do himself in." He complained of his homosexual tendencies, his poor relationship with his mother, his failures, his inability to get his life straightened out, and his sleepless nights as reasons to commit suicide. He once set himself on fire. Another time he overdosed on prescribed drugs. Doctors recommended involuntary commitment, but Ricky Lee always managed to get back out on the streets.

There, Ricky's social life was simple: visit friends, go to work, go to bars, and pick up kids. The instability of Ricky's life was particularly underscored by his job performance. Between June 1982 and September 1983 (just over one year), he worked at Lakeside Amusement Park, Thomas Joyland Shows (a carnival), a bottling company, an apparel company, restaurants, and cafeterias. Only once, at a printing company, did he hold a job longer than two to three months. Ricky explained that he quit the jobs after a short time because he didn't like them.

That Ricky's mental life was quickly deteriorating was especially evident by some of his practices and statements. He once built a fire because he wanted to "see Satan." He explained that he "plays both sides of the fence," worshipping God and Satan at different times. Unfortunately, he admitted, Satan "takes control" of his body most of the time. As early as 1979, six years prior to his conviction, he admitted looking forward to going to jail. He talked "about how he enjoys going to jail because of all the sexual activity available with frustrated incarcerated inmates." He also believed that "other people's thoughts control me," through thought broadcasting. And he made vague threats to doctors that he was "going to hurt somebody." So miserable was his home life that he determined "to live a life that will make it as miserable as hell for everybody."

Doctors described Ricky's activities as "anti-social," "violent," and "self-destructive." Throughout the years, doctors diagnosed his condition as "schizophrenia, paranoid type," "manic depressive illness, manic type," and said he suffered from "sexual maladjustment, and suicidal risk," and "sociopathic personality disorder."

And despite these compelling medical reports, the court placed fourteen-year-old Bruce in Ricky's home. What could Ricky think except that society was tolerating, if not approving, his pedophilia activities?

Deluded, Ricky continued his sexual assault against Bruce and other small children until a thirteen-year-old runaway shattered those delusions by telling police "everything."

"When Tommy came back to the apartment he said he told the police everything. I told Tommy, 'It's alright, I'm glad it's over.'"

A New Creature in Christ

After a year in prison, Ricky Lee has had some time to think: To think about the children he ravaged, the God he tried to exploit, and his life he destroyed.

"I'm in prison, but what about the boys?" he asked. "How will they know homosexuality is wrong? . . . I know for a fact they're not old enough to make rational decisions about their sex lives. The biggest majority don't even think a homosexual relationship is wrong. What makes one think they're going to change their decisions now? Some could grow up like David (a fifteen-year-old boy Ricky sexually abused) and decide they are a homosexual. And these may grow up to molest other children."

Though remorseful, Ricky doubted he would change his behavior toward young children if set free since Virginia state prisons do not offer medical help for inmates convicted of child molesting.

"You can send me to prison, but when I get out what's going to help me then? I feel that I cannot control my craving with juveniles. . . . If I get out of here, what's going to happen? Get caught and thrown back in here? Or have one of the parents kill me?"

He said, "I would rather remain in prison the rest of my natural life than to return to the streets and do this same perverted thing again."

But Ricky Lee is not without hope. "On May 31 at a prison in Powhatan I gave my life to the Lord."

He said, "I've been reading the Bible, particularly Leviticus, and God says homosexuality is wrong." And Ricky is convinced the Bible can "carry me through my enemies."

In a letter Ricky later sent, he wrote, "My faith in God assures me that He will make me a new creature in Christ Jesus. . . . And with God's help I will change. And I know that between me and my Creator, we know that I have changed. But for the sanity of those children (and the parents of some) that were my victims, it will be better if I remain in prison. Because I realize what those children really went through now. And I don't want them to fear that it would ever happen again."

SIX

A TEXTBOOK CHILD MOLESTER

Meredith S. may have been out of jail for five months, but he was still a prisoner of his sexual hunger for small children. Depraved, sinister, vicious, and treacherous—Meredith knew something terrible lay beneath his surface. "There is a monster in me," he admitted. "And I have been that monster. It's just not the face I show everybody." But on a particular March night in 1979, two children were about to meet that monster—that face which many a child had met before.

Meredith blamed stress. "I was under a lot of stress," he defended. "That's an excuse, I know. But I needed a release. I needed to get out from under the pressure. So I went out looking for some children."

Children? Why children?

"Because I needed to be in control," he answered. "When I was under stress I felt as though the world was controlling me, that I was being manipulated. But when I was molesting children I felt like I was the one in control, like I was the one doing the manipulating. It was a release. And on that night I needed a release."

The thirty-one-year-old Meredith did not look the part. His eyes were weak, not menacing. His medium build was flaccid, not rugged. And his face was oval, plump, and youthful, not gritting, perfidious, or diabolic.

With his charm, frequent smiles, and lamblike disposition, Meredith could have passed the scrutiny of the most dissecting parent—which he always did.

But beneath Meredith's superficial polish lay a demon—a demon that could transfigure Meredith into an ogre, into a child's quickening nightmare, into a whisper of death. A glance at Meredith's life is an unearthing of hell.

Relating the story, Meredith said he had been sitting in his 1970 hopped-up Mustang (which he bought because he knew it attracted children), when he contemplated where he might drive to pick up some kids. "I decided to go to the local 4-H Club," he said. "There are always children walking to the 4-H Club." With cocky self-assurance, Meredith raised his left eyebrow and added, "I never doubted whether I could pick up some kids."

A Turn to Violence

As he drove down an East Coast highway, Meredith stalked his prey and reflected on the past five months.

He had recently moved southward from New York, after a three-year prison stay, to start a new life. "I figured a new place would give me a new start."

But it didn't. When he arrived, Meredith happened upon a bar where he met a middle-aged drug-dependent woman—her scruples were a challenge even to Meredith's. Having drunk their alcohol, the two headed for home—her home. To Meredith's surprise—and delight—the woman had an eight-year-old son, Buddy. "Instead of ending up in bed with her," Meredith said, "I ended up in bed with him."

But unlike his other victims, Meredith was violent with Buddy. He slapped him, punched him, kicked him. "I used a lot of violence on him," Meredith said. "He was in lots of pain. He didn't like it, of course, but I didn't care." Neither did his mother care. All she wanted was her drugs—any drugs. "As long as I kept her supplied with drugs—anything I could lay my hands on that could give her a high—she was satisfied. She didn't care at all," Meredith recalled.

Meredith's sudden turn to violence was directly linked to his prison stay. "Make no mistake," Meredith said, "a child molester is not very well liked in prison. It's a cardinal sin behind bars as well as everywhere else."

While in the New York penitentiary, Meredith was pulled into a fight with an irate inmate who thought Meredith's punishment was more deserving of death than a three-year prison stay. Using a sharpened metal handle from a plastic bucket, the inmate lashed out at Meredith's face and chest. But Meredith avoided the thrusting strokes and parried long enough to pull out a similar weapon of his own. The two exchanged violent blows. But Meredith was the first to sustain a wound—a vicious laceration in the chest. It caught a bone, or else it might have punctured his lung. Before the pain registered, however, Meredith delivered an upper-cut that pierced the inmate under the left arm. It was a decisive blow, for there was no bone to stop the thin metal from penetrating deep into the inmate's shoulder.

Meredith survived this event, and prison life in general. But he made a vow: "When I get out, no child will ever tell on me again." Meredith was willing to kill rather than risk a child sending him back to prison.

So his violence against Buddy was a knee-jerk reaction to his fear of prison life. "Sure, there was some sexual pleasure. In fact I know there was," he said about Buddy's painful nights. "But it was primarily intended to put fear in him—to keep him from telling anybody outside what's going on inside."

Oddly enough, Meredith's conscience would not allow him to inflict pain on Buddy without "justification." As with most child molesters, Meredith had to persuade himself that he was doing nothing wrong: The pain was deserving, the sex desired. The child was always to blame. "For instance," he said, "to justify the pain I would break something, like pushing the boy into a lamp. Then I would accuse him of breaking the lamp and then justify to myself the need to beat him.

"I told myself for years that I was doing nothing wrong. If I knew I was doing something wrong, then I could never have done it."

The Catch

Out of prison, Meredith was back on the hunt for small children. Nothing much had changed—only that he was more violent, more suspicious, and more ruthless.

On the highway, the headlights of Meredith's Mustang finally reflected on his catch—two young boys walking that cool night on their way to the 4-H Club. Ready with his bait, Meredith pulled off the highway, threw the passenger door open, and yelled at the startled boys, "Hey, you kids seen my dog? He jumped out and I can't find him." The boys shook their head, looked around to see whether the dog had unsuspectingly maneuvered his way next to them, and said, "No. We haven't seen him."

"D--- dog," Meredith said in feigned disappointment. "Ah, never mind. He's probably gone for good this time. Hey, where you boys headed? You want a ride?"

"What do you say?" Roy asked Michael.

Michael resisted. He had heard the stories about madmen raping and killing kids. "No, let's walk," he said.

"Come on!" Roy demanded. "Let's go for a ride." They argued briefly. But the dispute ended when Roy got into the front seat and Michael got into the back.

For an hour and a half, Meredith drove the boys around. The two eleven-year-olds suspected nothing as they listened to rock music blaring from the car's eight speakers. Chatting among themselves, the boys occasionally tried to engage Meredith in a conversation. But Meredith would only "talk at them, not to them," because he was preoccupied: Where would he take the boys? How would he prevent them from telling anybody? Did he have the courage to rape them, beat them, or kill them if necessary? "My decision to molest them had been made," he said later. "But I had to put myself in a state of mind to carry it through."

By the time Meredith pulled into a gas station near an industrial center where he had once worked, his plan was formulated, his courage mustered, and his senses lost.

Driving deep into and through the industrial complex, Meredith stopped at its isolated outskirts. With ice building in his stomach, he looked at a set of railroad tracks barely noticeable on the moonlit night. Across these tracks, Meredith knew there lay a clearing.

Turning to Roy, Meredith said, "I got to go to the bathroom. Come on." But to Michael he ordered, "You sit there."

Michael refused. The night was much too dark, too foreboding, too mysterious for him to remain in the car by himself. Unwittingly, Michael exchanged the specter for the demon himself.

Standing in the clearing, Michael and Roy relieved themselves. Suddenly, a rush of pain filled their heads as they both fell toward the ground. Meredith explained, "I grabbed both of them over their mouths and rammed their heads together. I just wanted to shock them, to put fear in them."

As the boys looked up, they saw the "monster," the face which Meredith did not show everybody, but the face which many a child had seen before.

"Put your face on the ground," Meredith shouted at Michael. The boy obeyed immediately.

"Get up, Roy," the beast commanded. On legs that demurred and quaked, Roy straightened himself up. "Come here," he bellowed. The boy came. "Take off your clothes," the demon demanded. The boy refused.

With the back of his hand, Meredith delivered a forceful

blow across Roy's face. Then another blow. And another. Roy was paralyzed, a statue, a shell of a human being. He neither cried nor removed his clothes. He just stood there. So Meredith removed them for him.

Naked, Roy awaited the demon's next move. But there was none. Meredith just stared. And stared some more. Perhaps the monster was receding, perhaps the monster had a conscience. Meredith recalled, "My mind was willing, but my body was not. It probably had something to do with having to use force. I didn't *have* to use force before."

Turning away in disgust with himself, Meredith commanded the boy to get dressed.

Back in the car, the boys engaged in friendly conversation and talked as though nothing had ever happened. Actually the boys were afraid—afraid the demon would resurrect, afraid the demon might try again, afraid the demon might lash out and kill them. They wanted to say nothing that would give new life to this perishing spirit.

But Meredith found the mindless chatter disturbing. It wasn't supposed to be this way. Didn't they know their lives hung in the balance of a madman?

Once again his mind was preoccupied: Why could he not perform? Will the boys tell authorities? How could he silence them?

Pulling off the side of the road, across the street from where he picked them up, Meredith grabbed Roy's hair. Yanking it back to where Roy was forced to stare at the ceiling, Meredith looked intensely into the boy's horror-stricken eyes and said, "If you tell anybody, I'm going to kill you. Do you understand?" With as much movement as pain would allow, Roy nodded his head.

Roy kept his word and remained silent. But Michael never gave his word: He told.

Tracking Meredith down was simple. The gas station attendant had remembered that souped-up Mustang, and had remembered that it belonged to someone who used to work in the industrial park. After some interviewing, police found the hardware store where Meredith was once employed. Within hours the demon was in jail.

Meredith's sentence: ten years in jail. For some reason, he'd be free in six.

A Textbook Pedophile

Sitting in a "holding room" in a Virginia prison, Meredith described himself as a "textbook pedophile," which is quite a frightening statement considering his record of child abuse.

"I am the result of child sexual abuse," he defended. "I told, but they ignored me."

When Meredith was three years old he told his mother that his sixteen-year-old baby-sitter, Tom, was molesting him.

"Tom was a high school drop-out who lived in the neighborhood. He would baby-sit me while my mom worked," he recalled. "I remember the look on my mom's face when I told her. I remember watching the color drain from her face. But she did nothing about it, except to tell me not to let him do it anymore."

For the next year, until his parents moved away, Meredith was dropped each morning at Tom's house where he was molested almost daily.

Why did Meredith's mother continue to expose him to a child molester? "I don't think she believed me," he said. "It was too painful for her to admit that she had been dropping me off at a house where I was being sexually molested. What kind of mother would that be? So it was easier for her to ignore the charge as fanciful imagination on my part."

Then, when Meredith was seven years old, his thirteen-year-old sister started molesting him. "She would force me to perform various sexual acts. But because I was so young, some of the acts were impossible to do. So she would beat me. To control me she would give me alcohol and drugs." These sexual episodes were performed about every weekend for three years. "I didn't enjoy them, but she made threats that she would get me spanked or punished if I didn't cooperate."

Why didn't he tell his mother? "It didn't do any good the first time," he said convincingly.

When Meredith was eleven years old, he started molesting other children. He was not only physically capable, and not only primed for perverted sex, but he was a physical giant—standing nearly six feet tall and weighing 160 pounds—which allowed him to tower above his classmates and intimidate many into having sex.

Like most pedophiles, Meredith—even at this young age—calculated every major move around his desire for young children.

"I would steal money, mow lawns, shovel snow, rake leaves, and work at a secondhand shoe store, all as a means to an end—to use money to put young males into compromising positions," he said. "I was a con man.

"I never associated with children in my own age bracket. They were either older or younger," he said. "I hung around the older children because I was more in line with their activities—they were drug users, less inhibited, and drinkers. They were more apt to do the things I liked to do. And I hung around the younger kids because they could be easily manipulated into having sex."

Continuing to outline his strategy, he said, "I frequently fought with older kids. I was a bully. But, because of my size, I could be a bully. And when I would bully an older kid around this made younger kids more frightened and more apt to do what I wanted. They would say to themselves, 'If he beats big kids, then me too.' "

Nevertheless, Meredith lived in "tremendous fear" of being discovered as a "queer" by his peers. "That would have been devastating," he said. "I would walk down the school hall with stiff legs, I didn't want someone to see my buttocks moving. I was very conscious of doing anything that might be interpreted as feminine. . . . I didn't want to be called a faggot, a homosexual, or a queer, or any other popular name of the time."

During these school years, Meredith managed a steady sexual diet of young kids from age seven to fourteen years. "But with their tolerance, of course," Meredith clarified.

"I did want to be nice to these kids. I wanted them to like me, to respect me, to look up to me."

Meredith may have wanted to be admired by these abused children (in an egotistical sort of way), but he certainly had no feelings of love for those he sexually molested.

"Love wasn't something I thought a whole lot about. I was in love with myself, probably, but not with anyone else. I can't say I genuinely cared anything for an individual besides getting what I wanted from that individual," he said.

Meredith lacked love because he lacked trust. And if you trust no one, you love no one.

"I never trusted anybody. Why should I? I couldn't trust my mom. And if you can't trust your own mother, you can't trust anybody."

Meredith was raised in an upper-middle-class home. The youngest of two brothers and five sisters, he admitted to being spoiled. "If I complained enough, I always got what I wanted."

Determined to have his way in everything, Meredith grew in alienation and rebellion. "I remember thinking when I was nine years old how nice it would be to be an adult because nobody could force anything on me."

Recalling those rebellious years, he said, "I led an unhappy childhood. My parents pretty much ignored me because of my behavior. I was uncontrollable. . . . I was very, very firm in my belief that if it wasn't going to be my way, it wasn't going to be anybody's way."

After Meredith turned ten, his parents lost total control of him. He was arrested by police on several occasions, placed in a psychiatric hospital on several occasions, and confined to a reformatory on several occasions.

Predictably, Meredith's antisocial and sexually perverted behavior brought him into contact with society's dregs. He knew no fewer than fifty other New York pedophiles before his first arrest on child sex abuse charges.

It was through the meeting of one such pedophile that Meredith learned the true horror of his chosen lifestyle.

Child Pornographer or Child Killer?

Only nineteen years old at the time, Meredith had met Tom, a pedophile in his mid-forties, in Waverly, New York. A distinguished-looking man, Tom sported silver hair, flashy clothes, and a Lincoln Towncar. He was probably a child pornographer—or Meredith supposed.

"I was riding around the city with Tom one afternoon when he picked up a young boy hitchhiking," Meredith said. "Well, Tom looked at me and told me to drive. He said he was going to get in the back seat and that I was to drive back around and pick the boy up."

Meredith said he drove back around, powered the electric window down, and had asked the boy, "Where you headed? Do you want a ride?"

"I'm just bumming around," the boy had said, knowing that he was being propositioned by two pedophiles.

"Well, get in," Tom called from the back seat.

As the slender child climbed into the car, Tom asked, "What's your name?"

"Jimmy."

"Jimmy," Tom repeated, reaching into his wallet searching for a specific sum of cash. "Jimmy," he said, "here's a twenty dollar bill."

Though Jimmy was barely thirteen, the boy knew exactly what these men wanted. Never questioning the intent of the money, he removed his clothes.

Tom violated Jimmy. Then Jimmy violated Tom. But the ride was far from over.

Pulling out a $100 bill from his wallet, Tom slapped the greenback into Jimmy's hand and said, "Come back to my apartment."

Jimmy nodded; perhaps more sex, he supposed.

Tom's apartment was above a Waverly bar called The Brass Lantern. The flat was a rattrap. But Jimmy didn't seem to care. He asked only, "What do you want?"

"I want you to pose in pictures," Tom answered with a smile, knowing his prey was nibbling the bait.

The photo session began immediately. Jimmy removed his clothes. Tom snapped pictures in various stages of undress. And Meredith watched, without much interest, from the sidelines.

Suddenly there was a crash, a thud, the sound of two bodies flying to the floor. Meredith looked up. Tom had dived for Jimmy. He was obviously upset, but Meredith had no idea what the boy had done. Tom was like a madman. He was cursing at the boy, screaming in the child's face, beating him across the head. He yelled at the boy to scream back. But the boy was silent. Tom punched him, and punched him some more. But the boy said nothing. Finally, Tom threw the boy's head against the hard floor and stood up.

Meredith sighed in relief. Apparently Tom had cooled down, his anger spent, his composure regained—or so he hoped.

But turning to Meredith, Tom still showed great agitation and instructed, "Keep your eye on him. I'll be right back."

Tom headed off to the bedroom, but Meredith paid no attention. His eyes were glued to Jimmy, a young boy "earning" his one hundred dollars. He lay curled on the floor, crying, heaving, and—if he had sense—praying.

But before the boy could regain his senses, and before Meredith could put the pieces of the puzzle together, Tom called from the bedroom.

"Meredith, you and the boy come here."

Perhaps stunned, perhaps senseless, or perhaps terrified—the boy picked himself off the floor and followed Meredith's footsteps into the bedroom.

"Take off your pants," Tom commanded the boy, the lunatic now standing completely naked himself.

Jimmy started to obey. But before the child could put two fingers on his pants, Tom drove a fist deep into his stomach. The child doubled over.

Again, Meredith heard a crash, a thud, two bodies flying to the floor.

Tom then began a series of actions so violent and abusive they cannot be described in this book. By the time Tom had sated his perverse and vicious desire, the boy lay babbling, deep in shock.

Meredith stood lifeless, white, and dry.

"What are we going to do with him?" Meredith asked, more concerned about being part of a murder rap than the boy's welfare.

Tom looked at the boy with dry eyes. His solution was simple. With one hand, he grabbed a handful of hair and pulled the boy's head off the floor. With the other hand, he grabbed a handful of steel and pulled the gun off the edge of the bed.

"Well hell," he said to Meredith, "let's just put a bullet in his head and go dump him."

"You can't do that," Meredith said quickly, his heart beating rapidly, feeling its thumping in his throat.

"Sure I can." And pointing the barrel at the boy's head, Tom squeezed the trigger.

"Wait a minute!" Meredith shouted, on the verge of uncontrollable tears. "Don't do it. Don't kill him."

Tom hesitated, his finger relaxing slightly, the gun's hammer head receding gently.

"Let me take the kid somewhere," Meredith said in heaving sobs. "I'll dump him."

Shaking like a reed in the wind, Meredith inched closer to the lunatic, pleading mercifully as he crept.

Fearful that at any moment the smell of gunfire could fill the room, Meredith grabbed the boy's arm and began pulling slightly.

"Come on, man. Please. Give me your keys. Let me take him somewhere."

Looking at Meredith, then looking at the boy again, Tom pointed the gun to a pair of pants lying across the bed and said, "They're in my pants. Take the keys and get the boy out of here."

Where Meredith had dumped the boy he could not remember. "All I can remember is that it was by a green house with yellow shutters." But once dumped, Meredith brought the car back to the Waverly bar, tossed the keys under the seat, and caught the first bus to New York City and got "out of Dodge."

Breeding Other Pedophiles

The experience was terrifying, its every detail engraved in his memory. But rather than turn his back on his perverted lifestyle, Meredith continued in his child molestings.

Using mental gymnastics, Meredith convinced himself that he was simply catering to the sexual needs and desires of the children.

He explained, "I denied that I was the one who instigated it. I would tell myself, 'You're not doing anything wrong. You're just doing what they want you to do.' That made it liveable."

Before Meredith turned twenty-one he had molested over 150 children. He was particularly attracted to boys from eleven to fourteen years. But he had abused children even younger, the youngest being but four years old.

These numbers are shocking. But even more shocking is the number of children that were previously molested even before Meredith laid a hand on them.

"The amount of kids that I have had that were sexually abused prior to me will astound the senses," Meredith said. "And I fear that a rather high percentage of these abused kids will grow up to abuse other kids because many of the children I abused wanted repeated sex. In fact, I had one child who was like glue."

Meredith estimated that as many as one-half of the children he had molested had had anal intercourse before his abuse. He said probably one-half of these will grow up to be homosexuals. And as many as one in five will grow up to be pedophiles like himself.

Such a statement is astounding. If Meredith is correct, thirty children that he has molested are now combing the streets of New York City, molesting other children, and making future pedophiles.

It was precisely this thought, that he was creating other pedophiles, that caused Meredith to admit that his perverted activities were wrong and destructive to children.

"I began to become disappointed with my life in about 1980," he said. "It started after watching a movie called *Fallen Angel*. It was about a pedophile who nearly destroyed a young girl's life that he had been molesting. Well, the movie changed my life. I said to myself, 'They're just kids. What are they going to be like when they grow up?' I never felt so much hate for myself in all my life. And the effects still haven't worn off."

Shortly afterwards, Meredith viewed another program that forced him to examine his depravity.

"I was watching 'Lou Grant'—you know, the program where he plays an editor of a newspaper. Well, this particular episode was about a nine-year-old girl being prostituted by her mother. When the girl was later interviewed by a reporter, there was no life in her eyes. She was like walking death. It scared me. It made me think I was creating monsters. And I knew I was. When I was young and my sister molested me, and my neighbor molested me, I hated it. Yet, there I was molesting other children, making them go through the very same thing I hated.

"I was creating an atmosphere for more Merediths in the world," he said. "I'm not really pleased with myself. And I don't want anybody to go through what I've gone through."

With self-disgust, he said, "There's not a day in my life I haven't thought about what I've done. And there isn't a day in my life I haven't thought about taking the easy way out—suicide.

"And I will be dead before it ever happens again."

Wanting to Help

Four years ago, Meredith would have kept those dark secrets to himself—his vile behavior was no one else's business. His actions were wrong, he knew. But he also felt he had been wronged by society when he was a child. He felt no need, therefore, to expose his disfigured and vulgar life to the public. But that was four years ago. Now, conscience-stricken, Meredith is anxious to redeem himself, or at least try. Believing redemption lies in his willingness to help parents protect their children, Meredith detailed the strategies of a child molester—the most vital ingredient in knowing how to protect the child.

For Meredith, locating children to sexually abuse was simple: Find children from poor home environments, convince them they are old enough to make adult decisions about sex, and threaten them with embarrassment, harm, or death if the secret is told.

"I looked for the kid who didn't have a real good home life—the kid with the devil-may-care attitude," he said. "Most of the kids I molested were neighbors, but they weren't from stable homes. They got away with things like staying out late at night and smoking cigarettes. They weren't necessarily defiant, just looking for attention.

"I didn't have much trouble finding them. I just chose the boys who acted and behaved like myself."

Traditional hangouts for pedophiles include parks, schools, shopping malls, bus stations, department stores, public bathrooms, swimming pools, churches, and grocery stores.

Explaining some of these, Meredith said elementary schools represent the greatest risk to children because "many pedophiles have houses in the neighborhood so they can explain their presence in the area."

Public bathrooms are "excellent places for pedophiles to go and watch the child while he urinates. But it's like window-shopping. You look, but you don't touch."

Surprisingly, for those pedophiles who do not live next to a school, the best place to "hang out" is at grocery stores. "Especially grocery stores," Meredith said, "because mothers don't take their kids in shopping with them. It was nothing to start conversations with these kids and find out something about their family or where they live. You would be amazed at the number of parents who leave their children, many of them under ten, unattended in the cars."

For the same reasons, swimming pools are frequent hangouts for pedophiles. "Because most parents don't take their children to public swimming pools, I would often sit in the locker room and watch the children undress. It was a very easy place to make friends."

Churches were particularly convenient for picking up children. "Churchgoers are gullible," Meredith said. "I've met many children this way."

A Wolf in Sheep's Clothing

Meredith, explaining this gullibleness among church members, said he frequented one church and, knowing how much the congregation appreciated a person who gives up his time to perform custodial work, volunteered to keep the church clean. Winning the respect and admiration of the pastor and congregation, Meredith succeeded in presenting himself as a devout Christian and religious worker.

Once the congregation was deceived, Meredith was ready to make his move: He volunteered to move two soda machines and scrub the brown filth off the floor which was left behind. "I simply told the preacher, 'Hey, give me a couple of boys and I'll do this job right.'" The pastor, of course, did just that.

Alone in the church building with the boys, Meredith sent one child out to the store for some snacks and additional scrubbing material.

He then placed his arm around the other boy and told him to go into the bathroom, that there was something he wanted to show him. The boy questioned the request, but obeyed nevertheless. Inside the restroom, Meredith turned out the lights and literally raped the child.

Then, *to Meredith's shock,* the child said, "Boy, I've had sex with other men, but I've never been raped like that before."

"I couldn't believe it," Meredith said. "Even in a church setting, I was molesting children who had been molested before."

Screening the Child
Going to a traditional hangout and finding unsupervised, defiant children was easy, Meredith said. But this was not enough evidence that a child could be easily molested.

To determine whether a child could be easily molested, Meredith needed to screen the child.

"I got to know the kid. I got to know his family. I would ask the child, 'What're your parents' first names?' 'What does your dad do for a living?' 'What's your phone number and address?' 'Does your dad play ball with you?' Well, if a child hasn't been taught his phone number or address, and his home relationship is so poor that he doesn't even know his parents' first names or where his dad works, and if his father doesn't play ball with him, this child is vulnerable."

Meredith said he would also pay attention to a child's dress—whether clean and neat or ragged and sloppy. There were even such intangible indicators as a child's demeanor.

But having determined a particular child is vulnerable, Meredith's plan was then simple: Do the things a father should do. Become the closest human being in that child's life—be his friend, play ball with him, give him money, small gifts and pets, help him through his problems, defend his interests, show him such emotional display as hugging.

Then, using a type of peer pressure, Meredith would attempt to convince the child that he is old enough to make adult decisions about sex. If the child complains that he is too young for sex, Meredith accuses the boy of being a "baby." And since no child likes to be belittled by an adult, especially when the child leans toward the defiant life and comes from a poor home relationship, the strategy usually worked.

Describing this strategy in action, Meredith told how he would hang out in the parks during the summer months waiting for mothers to drop off their unsupervised children.

"I would sit on the park bench feeding bread crumbs to the birds. To the parents, I looked very unsuspecting. But to the kids—when they discovered my radio and my bag of dope—I looked very attractive.

"Marijuana was a big catch. They would come over and ask for some, but I would tell them they're too young. They, of course, would deny this and tell me how old they are, that they've done it before. Well, they were falling right into my plan, of course. I was trying to psyche them into thinking they're mature. By belittling them as children, I was—at the same time—making them want to prove me wrong. So I would make them ask me for money and marijuana. Or, in other situations, I would make them ask me for a beer or to drive my car—anything to make them think they were mature and capable of making and performing adult decisions.

"After I've hooked the child into thinking that he's an adult, I would pop the question, 'How about a little sex?' Most would say no. But I would follow the refusal by asking if they thought their parents had sex, which, of course, they would say yes. But the kids defended their parents' right to do so because they were adults. Then I would say, 'Oh, that's right. You're just a kid, a baby. You're not able to make an adult decision.' This put them on the defensive because they knew if they weren't an adult they couldn't smoke any more marijuana, drink any more beer, or drive my car. So they would break down and say they were adult enough to have sex."

There were times when Meredith did not feel like going through such exhaustive psychological games with the children and he would simply slip the child a "mickey"—some knock-out drops acquired at local drugstores—and rape the child as he lay unconscious.

Silencing the Child
Keeping the child silent about sex was little problem.

"I would tie two cat tails together and throw them over a clothesline. The cats would claw themselves to death. Then I would tell the child, 'The same thing will happen to you if you tell.' Sometimes I would put a firecracker in a frog's mouth and make the child watch its head blow up. Then I'd tell him the same thing will happen to his family if he tells."

He added, "But most of the time, I only needed to hurt their feelings. I'd say, 'If you tell, you just wait till we get to court and I'll make you look like a bitch. You don't think others will believe you didn't want to do it, do you? I didn't make you open your mouth. I didn't make you pull your pants down.' It would scare the hell out of any child who didn't want to be known as a homosexual."

How well did such threats work? "I've molested more than 150 children and I've only been told on twice, so what do you think?" Meredith answered sarcastically.

But more importantly than threats, Meredith said, is having selected a child from a poor home life. "That's why most pedophiles don't get told on," he said. "The child would rather receive the interest than tell. They feel that's satisfying a need for them."

The Best Advice
Meredith's advice to parents, then, is obvious: Make sure the child has a good home life.

"I stayed away from the kid who knew his parents' names and phone number, or who says his father taught him baseball. You don't even want to be near a boy who has a good relationship with his parents."

Ironically, these are also the children who might end up dead, Meredith said.

"If a child comes from a good home life, he better also be taught to go along with the child molester. If he is put into the position, he should be taught to cooperate. For as soon as you give the molester the impression you don't want to go along you become a threat to him. You're going to tell. And he's going to kill you. Besides, some pedophiles love a fighter, and these are the kids who end up dead in the woods."

Meredith said the solution is to teach the child how not to be put in the position of having to cooperate. "Don't get into the car, the house, or the garage."

Salvation Afar
Though repentant, Meredith was not sure whether he could change his ways once outside prison. "If I went out to the streets tomorrow, I would be back. Why? Because it's the way I deal with stress.

"You don't quit being a pedophile," he said. "I will always want a child. But I must develop other tastes."

Then, as though he had given great consideration to this problem, he said, "I think I will settle upon homosexuality."

But what about AIDS?

"I would rather people say, 'Oh, there goes a homosexual with AIDS,' than, 'Oh, there's a pedophile who goes around abusing little boys,' " Meredith said.

Perhaps. But this is not the only alternative. He could try to develop a proper relationship with a girl.

"That would be too hard," he said. "I've never been sexually attracted to girls. It would be too risky, unnatural."

And what about Jesus Christ. Has he ever thought of giving his life over to his Creator, asking Him for salvation, asking Him for redemption? Jesus Christ could set him free from this bondage.

"Do you know when I stopped believing in Jesus Christ?" Meredith asked emphatically as resentment built in his eyes. "The day my sister molested me."

SEVEN

THE FORCES BEHIND CHILD SEXUAL ABUSE

A scientific explanation for the rise in child sexual abuse does not exist. Social scientists have not yet answered the question, How bad? to consider the greater question, Why?

But we are not without clues.

Since the pedophile has not attempted to cover his tracks, his trail provides a host of reasons for the increase in child sexual abuse.

Tracing those footsteps backwards, we find two great social upheavals that plowed the ground for the current decade of child sexual abuse: the sexual revolution of the 1960s and the Me Generation of the 1970s. The sexual revolution "liberated" society from sexual taboos which gave child sex abusers a right to exist, organize, and practice this perversion. The Me Generation resulted in broken homes, alienated youth, and an overall devaluation of children which psychologically primed children for sexual abuse by adults.

It must be understood, however, that the rise in child sexual abuse did not occur simultaneously with these two great upheavals, but rather trailed a few years behind. Like scavengers following a flood, child sexual abusers neither caused, nor took part in, the sexual revolution or the Me Generation that

wreaked so much moral damage. But, after the land was laid
waste, these foul sexual practitioners followed and took advantage of society's morally weakened state to inflict additional
abuse on our children.

The Sexual Revolution

"Just as we strive to free young people from the
tyranny of 'Thou Shalt Not,' so we must free them
from the tyranny of 'Thou Shalt!' We must make
them truly free because no weight of statistics or
percentages can dictate what moral choice a person
shall make." Rev. William Genne, founder of Sex
Information and Education Council (1964).[1]

"Whether an act is moral or immoral is determined
by the 'law of love;' that is the extent of which love
and concern for others is a factor in the relationship." Arthur E. Gravatt, M.D., and leading sex education proponent.[2]

Until the early 1960s, child sex abusers were socially
stigmatized. The nation held traditional moral beliefs, meaning
the social consensus viewed sex outside of marriage as wrong.
This standard, rooted in the Biblical command against fornica-
tion and adultery, proved a barrier even for the heterosexually
promiscuous and homosexual, and all the more for the child
sex abuser.

But under the "new morality," pedophilia has gained a
legitimate claim to existence.

The "new morality" is the handiwork of Dr. Joseph
Fletcher, the father of situation ethics, and other moral philosophers. Dr. Fletcher (and crew) is responsible for society dis-
pensing with "pre-cooked ethics" (a term he used to refer to
Biblical rules of conduct) in favor of ethical humanism.

Dr. Fletcher has argued, "We cannot continue to turn

simplistically to the teachings of Moses or Jesus or Mohammed for direct ethical guidance. Things are just not that simple anymore."[3]

Explaining ethical humanism (which has successfully supplanted Biblical morality as today's guidelines for moral behavior), Dr. Fletcher states, "What justifies an act is its results, not its conformity to moral rules."[4]

"In short," he said, "everything depends upon the consequences."[5]

Another leading moral philosopher, Eike-Henner Kluge, has also explained the new morality. He writes, "Doing your own thing is alright, so long as you don't bother anyone, and so long as you are indeed doing something which is valuable or leads to a situation that you value or deem to be valuable at the present time."[6] In other words, he explained, "What we feel is right goes."[7]

Applying the new morality to sexual practices, moral philosophers propose these rules: Sexual intercourse is an acceptable practice as long as, (1) the partner is willing, (2) it is done out of respect (some say love), and (3) it is not irresponsible—meaning safeguards are taken to prevent pregnancy.

A Morality Without Boundaries
Such a morality, however, not only makes room for the adulterer, the promiscuous, and the homosexual, but for the child sex abuser as well. For the "new morality" does not erect any logical boundaries to prevent the child molester from having a right to exist.

That is, the child molester can easily claim that his sex is with a consenting child, performed as an act of love, and without the risk of pregnancy.

An editorial in a child pornography magazine even argued this very view. Wrote Edward Brongersma, a former member of the Upper House of the Dutch Parliament, "We have come to the conclusion that the term 'indecent' can no longer be used to include sexual behavior which arises through love, tenderness or affection and which is not carried out against the will of the child."[8]

The "new morality," then, may not have invited the child molester on the trip, but it is certainly incapable of preventing him from boarding the bus. The new moral standard is open-ended enough to justify his existence.

Within recent years, the liberal moralist has revised his definition of permissive sex to counter the claims of pedophiles. The new guideline states, "Sex is acceptable only between consenting *adults*." But the revision has been both inconsistent and lacking logic.

That is, the guideline is inconsistent because the liberal moralist still believes sex between consenting children is acceptable (as long as contraception is practiced), and the guideline is without logic because it fails to adequately explain why sex between adults and children is wrong. The official explanation is that children are not old enough to make a mature decision about having sex with an adult. Yet, if this were true—and consistently practiced—the child would not be old enough to make a mature decision about having sex with another child as well. But to state this position would be to blow a hole in the new morality and destroy liberal moralists' sex education programs. For the "new morality" teaches children not to feel guilty about having sex. Why? The liberal moralist believes that if the child does not feel guilty about having sex, he or she will not feel guilty about obtaining contraceptives, which, he believes, is the only acceptable solution to illegitimate pregnancies. To claim sex between children is wrong would be to impose guilt, and this would defeat the liberal moralist solution to out-of-wedlock pregnancies.

As sex-ed guru Peter Scales states, "We can't help some people say 'no' to potential sexual partners . . . if we're telling all young people to say 'no' to sex itself . . . [we want them to get to the point that] when they say 'yes,' it will be with carefully chosen partners, with respect for themselves and their partners which will require them to be prepared [i.e., obtain contraceptives]. . . . The lesson of sex education is clear: though education can encourage responsible sexual behavior, it will not help reduce V.D. and unwanted pregnancy if we continue to lace teenage sexual behavior with a good dose of guilt, fail to break down myths of 'normal' sexuality and neat sex-role differences, make it difficult for young people to use sexual health care services, and comfort ouselves with the destructive notion that 'ignorance is bliss.' "[9] So the "new morality" must be sufficiently versatile to permit guiltless sex between children.

The Slippery Slope

Unable to denounce sex between children as wrong, then, the liberal moralist is only able to erect an artificial barrier against the child sexual molester. Like a frustrated parent who yells at a very demanding child, "No, because I said so," the liberal moralist is only able to deny the child molester his sex with children by claiming, "No, because we say so." But this artificial barrier is without the moral strength of logic to deter child sexual abuse because the "new morality" actually permits sex between adults and children.

The "new morality" is an excellent example of the "slippery slope" argument.

The slippery slope argument says that once society forsakes eternal truths it will slide ever downward into more degenerate practices.

In the current case, society rejected God's truths that it forsake sex outside of marriage. It then constructed a "new morality" that said sex between consenting partners is acceptable. But the argument stepped onto the "slippery slope" and, as a result, allowed even child molesters to legitimize their practices. To prevent this downward slide, the liberal moralist resorted to constructing an artificial barrier that said only sex between consenting adults is permissible. But being only an artificial, illogical, and inconsistent barrier, the "new morality" was incapable of preventing its downward slide into the hands of the child sex molester.

Therefore, whether the liberal moralist admits it or not, the "new morality" has given the child molester a legitimate right to exist in society. Having stepped onto the slippery slope, the moralist is unable to construct a "new morality" that allows promiscuous sex, adolescent sex, and homosexual sex, yet, at the same time, forbids sex between adults and children.

But perhaps Ricky Lee (who reasoned that if society permits "abnormal" sex between adults, why not children?) explained the slippery slope best when he said, "If you give somebody an inch they're going to take a mile."

Call It Anything But Sin
Another area legitimizing the existence of child sex abusers are laws designed to prohibit discrimination against homosexuals. These laws, which have passed in more than fifty states, counties, or cities, invariably prohibit people from being discriminated against because of their "sexual orientation," or "sexual preference." The sponsors of the laws—preferring euphemisms over the word "homosexual"—have created laws that beg permission to sit on the "slippery slope." For who can deny the child sex molester that his perversion is also a "sexual preference" or "sexual orientation?" And along this same line, the euphemism "making love" is another example of a slippery slope argument. A term originally intended to justify promiscuous sex (by arguing that the sex is out of respect and love), "making love" fits neatly into the child molester's vocabulary and allows him to perceive a social right to exist since he too is only "making love."

Child Sex in Popular Culture
And permission for the child sex molester to exist does not end here. The arts and entertainment culture has been especially

culpable in this area with its frequent display of children as being sexual, sensual, mature, and promiscuous. And this would include those product manufacturers who commercialize the sexuality of children to sell their goods—jeans advertisers being the most visual and reprehensible in this area.

But jeans companies are not the only reputable manufacturers showing great insensitivity toward child sexual abuse. As an example, on June 5, 1984, U.S. Customs seized one hundred record albums manufactured by RCA as a possible violation of child pornography statutes. The albums, imported from the Netherlands and mailed to Scorpio Music, Inc., in Philadelphia were produced by the rock recording group, the Scorpions. The front cover of the album jackets displayed a naked girl, about ten years old, with shattered glass accenting her pubic area. She was sprawled out beneath the title, *Virgin Killer*.[10]

With "respectable" manufacturers flaunting the sexuality of children, should it come as a surprise that pedophiles feel society has given them the right to exist?

And let's not forget Hollywood. When television producers are not writing sitcoms that show children struggling with sexual hangups, its movie producers are showing adolescents as having an insatiable curiosity, lust, exploration, or love for sex—*Boarding School, Foxes, Endless Love, The Blue Lagoon, Sweet Young Thing, The Last American Virgin, Private School, Hot Times, My Tutor, Porky's,* and *Private Lessons* are but a *few* such movies.

The film *Blame It On Rio* (which featured the highly regarded actors Michael Caine and Joseph Bolgna) even had the brassness to take the "legitimate" film industry to the borders of moral limits by making sport of two fathers trying to initiate sex with the daughter of the other. (Not to mention, of course, the films *Pretty Baby* and *Lolita* which were discussed in Chapter One.)

These films, of course, are not attempting to produce pedophiles. They are attempting to make money, primarily from the youth market. Nevertheless, their films are not without social consequences. First, they support the pedophile's argument that children are sensual creatures yearning for sex. Second, the films send a social signal to the pedophile that adolescent sex is not only acceptable, but suitable material to be featured in films and exploited for entertainment. Third, they feed the perverted sexual drives of child molesters. And fourth, the films teach children that it is natural to engage in impulsive sex—an education of great benefit to pedophiles.

This fourth point should not be taken lightly. Youth are frequently besieged with messages of sex. Movies, television, music, peer pressure, advertisements, even curriculum materials in some public schools—all bombard the youth with the idea that sex, love, and sensuality are essential ingredients to popularity, adulthood, acceptance, style, maturity, and self-fulfillment. In other words, many social forces conspire together to try to forge the child into a valueless sexual creature. How can the pedophile not capitalize on such pressure and indoctrination?

Child Sex in "Adult" Pornography

But probably the most important endorsement of society on the right of child sex molesters to exist is its tolerance of the "adult" pornography industry and its explicit depictions of adolescent and child sex.

Unlike the child pornographer, which society rejects (at least with lip service), the adult pornographer is accepted by the social establishment. Civil libertarians, lawmakers, the courts, the media, and the medical community—all speak highly about the need and right of pornographers to market their goods. If, therefore, it can be demonstrated that the adult pornography industry promotes child sexual abuse, then society must accept the blame for not only—once again—giving the child molester a right to exist, but for promoting his abuse of children as well.

Complete Denial

The adult pornography industry, it should be noted, denies that it endorses child sex.[11]

"The adult entertainment industry is not associated with child sex," porn actress Tish Ambrose told me. Her colleagues were just as adamant. Said Al Goldstein, publisher of a New York pornography tabloid, "I am opposed to showing children as sex objects. . . . The Adult Film Association has fought all films dealing with pedophilia and it has even contributed money to help locate missing children." Said porn actor Marc Stevens, who has appeared in over six hundred such films, "The only thing adult film makers oppose showing in their films is anything involving children. And we always felt that. I'm totally against that." Said Gloria Leonard, publisher of the pornography magazine *High Society*, "Independently we've all denounced that sort of kinky stuff." And at the Critics Adult Film Awards held in New York in 1985, many directors, actors, actresses, screen-writers, etc., ridiculed the use of children in sex scenes.

But one New York adult film distributor and theatre owner said, "Off the record, they're lying."

Overwhelming Evidence

Let's look at the facts.

During a one-week period in May 1985, these child-oriented film clips were being shown in New York City's video-peep booths (a video-peep booth is a small, closet-size private booth that has a television monitor or screen inside and which shows a five- to ten-minute film clip of an explicit sex scene): "Teenage Sex," "Schoolgirl Education," "First Date," "Loves of Lolita," "Music for Teens," "English Schoolgirls," "Teenage Climax," and "Grandfather's Love."

Also during the same week, these adolescent-oriented feature films were available in New York City (feature films are generally ninety minutes in length and are shown inside X-rated theaters): *Private School Girls, Panty Raid, New Wave Hookers, Young Girls Do,* and *Sweet Foxes.*

And these are just the films whose predominant theme revolves around adolescent sex. There were other films available which depicted adolescent sex at least once.

With the many child and adolescent sex films available in just one city—during just one week—how can the pornography industry claim it does not endorse child sex? And, if the industry is so interested in denouncing child sexual abuse, why does it insist on producing films that glamorize child sex?

Industry officials are not without answers. To the first question, they deny that child sex is endorsed in their films since all of their actors and actresses are models over eighteen years of age, even though the performers are cast in roles portraying minors. To the second question, they say films dealing with child or adolescent sex merely provide a product the customer obviously enjoys. And since the industry denies the use of underaged performers and denies that the films cause the customer to want to repeat the sex act, they do not believe their films endorse child sexual abuse.

Porn screenwriter and producer Joyce Snyder explained, "The industry is just trying to satisfy an audience. Men feel old. Young girls make them feel young. They don't ask for a commitment, they're not demanding, they just want a good time. It's not a conspiracy to violate young girls. It's a fantasy trip to have these promiscuous, undemanding girls available. Men want to fantasize that women are available, loose, and wanting to have sex. Young girls fit this bill."

(Some industry officials, however, think the porn establishment should avoid adolescent sex themes in their movies. Said Howard Farber, president of Vid-X-Pix (a producer of X-rated films), "We have made movies showing sex with older women. The younger girls are really not that sexual. A lot of men like to fantasize about having sex with younger girls. But the industry should steer clear of teen sex. I've even turned down a film that would have a girl in pigtails in a high school setting." And Al Goldstein, publisher of the New York porn tabloid *Screw* said, "We don't know whether portraying adults as children in a sex scene creates a clientele for that sort of thing. But showing girls as minors in a sexual situation has been here all along. It distresses me. Some of these films even have the girl's pubic hair shaved to make them look younger. From a moral point of view we should have adults having sex with adults. That would be a statesmanlike position.")

Child sex is also promoted in "adult" pornography magazines.

"Adult" bookstores offer a variety of titles designed to titillate the pedophile, or those individuals close to becoming pedophiles. A list of such titles include: *Young and Lonely, Virgin Love, Baby Dolls, Young Love, Young Darlings, Little Loving Dolls, Young Girls.* Of course there are other titles too graphic to mention here, but they typically begin with words like *young, teen, peachfuzz, tender,* or *baby.* The magazines, without exception, sport a very young looking girl on the cover in a setting that obviously depicts adolescence—or even pre-adolescence. And, if this is not enough to prompt a sale, the magazines carry teaser headlines describing the cover girls as oversexed nymphets. "Sex secrets of the young and wild ones," reads one. "School Girl Nymph," reads another. "Men will do until the right dog comes along," flaunts a third. "Flaming young lovers in search of the mature man," another boasts. Inside the magazines, of course, are explicit shots of young girls who tell their tales of sex with older men.

Child Sex in "Established" Erotica
But these off-the-wall magazines are not the only porn publications promoting children as sexual objects. Such "established" porn monthlies as *Playboy, Penthouse, Hustler,* and *Oui* also endorse the sexuality of children.

Oui even carries advertisements for child sex publications and movies in its magazines (though, in reality, these films and magazines may only use psuedo-children—that is, girls over eighteen years of age who have the appearance of minors).

In *Oui's* March 1985 issue alone, it carried advertisements for such movies as *Teen Orgy, Schoolgirl, Daddy's Darling Daughter, Mother in the Middle, Teenage Gang Bang, School Doctor, Father Knows Best, Hi School Honies,* and *Little Anal Annie.* Advertised magazines include *Teen Cream Puffs, Young Wild. . . . ,* and *Teeny Twatters.*

The same magazine also carried these personal ads: "Pictures of my 4 girls: New censorship restrictions on magazine publishers prevent me from telling you how old they are or what my girls are doing in them. You can't get this kind of stuff from the big dealers any more." "Love drops are a must for the man who has difficulty getting women to cooperate. . . . Works on *young girls* or older women. . ." (emphasis supplied). "Turkish Porno. . . . See unbelievable acts of every kind, every age." "Free! . . . 16 glossy photos from new films made esp. (sic) for 'young stuff' collectors. . . ." "My two nasty girls. . . . I can't mention ages in this ad, but our home movies and pictures are better than the commercial stuff!" "Mama's Sex. She's overcome by the delivery boy. . . ."

But child sex themes in *Oui* are not new. As far back as August 1975, the magazine made light of child sexual abuse. In an advertisement placed in *Playboy,*[12] *Oui* billed its 1975 child sex segment as follows: "How one family solved its discipline problem." (Above this text is a still photo of a young nymphet sitting nude and spread-eagle on a sheetless mattress. The white framed bedpost is battered, as though struck quite frequently by a hard object. Its chipped paint gives the photograph a violent appearance. But probably more striking are the handcuffs that immobilize the girl's hands.) "This is Jane," the copy reads. "When she is nice, she is very, very nice. But when she is naughty, she has to be punished. Lately, Jane has been very, very naughty. That's why, in the current issue of *Oui* magazine, Jane is pictured in a variety of poses that restrict her movement. It was movement that got Jane into trouble in the first place. So you see, it's for her own good. And not incidentally, your pleasure."

But what about the nation's three top-selling erotic magazines—*Playboy, Penthouse, Huster*—do they really promote child sexual abuse?

A History of Promoting Child Sex
In *Playboy's* thirty-one-year history, the magazine featured children in its cartoons 1,196 times (from December 1954 to December 1984). In *Penthouse's* fifteen-year history, the magazine featured 265 child cartoons (September 1969 to December 1984). And in *Hustler's* ten-year history, the magazine featured 555 child cartoons (July 1974 to December 1984). The combined efforts of these three magazines has resulted in 2,016 child cartoons. And the largest group of children by age is 636 cartoons of youngsters aged six to eleven years old![13]

Though the children are not always portrayed in a sexual situation (sometimes they simply observe sex, participate in violence, or are just a character in a non-violent, non-sexual setting), the total number of cartoons where children were either the initiator or recipient of sex is a startling 1,142 times. (Children were displayed in violent cartoons 712 times.) Both the sexual and violent cartoons condone the abuse and disrespect of children.

The content of these cartoons, ever since 1954, have always been graphic, repugnant, uninhibited, insulting, and defiant. A sampling of the years include:

Playboy June 1954, a boy of five years is watching an old man having sex with a young woman. The old man tells the child, "Here's a quarter to stick around. I may need your help later."

Penthouse December 1977, Santa Claus pumps a dozen

bullets into a tot and says to the dead child lying in a pool of blood, "That'll teach you to be a good boy."

Playboy January 1977, Santa Claus wipes blood off his fanged mouth and tells his helper, "Bring in another!"

Hustler April 1979, two young boys have a small girl pinned to the floor. Mother walks in to find the young girl screaming her head off because a vacuum cleaner hose is crammed up her vagina. One of the boys says, "Relax, Mom, we're just playing abortionist."

Hustler December 1976, an obstetrician delivers a child and then smashes its head between his hands. He tells the mother, "So you can't pay your bill, heh, Mrs. Jones?"

Hustler June 1976, a naked five-year-old girl looks up to a puzzled oil sheik and says, "Hi, mister. If you promise to give me one of your oil wells, I'll let you play with my pee-pee."

Penthouse November 1976, a small girl holding a candy cane tells her playmates, "Yeah! and he gives you one of these, just for straight sex, no deviations!"

Hustler April 1977, a cartoon called "Chester the Molester" depicts Little Red Riding Hood walking to Grandmother's house. Behind a tree waits a man with a baseball bat, the wolf is hanging by his neck from a limb.

The Wizard of Oz is an apparent favorite among the erotic magazines. In 1968 *Playboy* ran a cartoon of Dorothy sitting on the Yellow Brick Road with the wicked witch lustfully saying, "Would you like to know what I *really* want?" (emphasis theirs). Ten years later, *Playboy* ran another Land of Oz cartoon with Dorothy again sitting on the Yellow Brick Road. This time she has just been raped and pointing to the Scarecrow and the Tin Man she tells an onlooking policeman, "That's them, officer!" And in November 1982, *Hustler* embellished the Land of Oz even further by bringing life to the characters. In what must have been an extremely expensive photographic layout spread called "The Land of Ahhs," Dorothy becomes the sexual servant in a "gang bang" involving the Lion, the Tin Man, and the Scarecrow. (The pictorial even had the Scarecrow urinating in Dorothy's mouth which, by the way, is a favorite activity among child molesters.)

Penthouse December 1977, the seven dwarfs stand next to Snow White as she lies sleeping on a bed. One dwarf says to the others, "All those in favor of a gang bang say 'Hi Ho.'"

Penthouse September 1978, a doctor tells Peter Pan, "I've got bad news, Peter. Tinker Bell has got the clap!"

Hustler April 1977, a high school girl is being sexually molested by her father. She tells her dad, "Daddy, not only is what you're doing illegal, it's being done badly."

Playboy May 1974, a naked girl lies in bed with an elderly bearded man and tells her mother over the phone, "Everything's fine, Momma. Uncle William and I are playing a game called consequences."

These samplings of cartoons are not meant to be gratuitous but to show the reader that the nation's top three erotic magazines use young children and their fairy tales to portray youngsters as enjoying sex with other children and with adults and as the object of extreme violence.

Though these cartoons were infrequent when *Playboy* released its first issue in 1954 (less than ten cartoons each year), by 1982 the number of cartoons depicting children as the recipient or initiator of sex or violence in the three magazines rose to more than 120 cartoons each year.

Pseudo-Children

With the rise of children in cartoons came a rise of pseudo-children in photographic layout spreads. These elaborate photo sessions are painstakingly shot to depict young girls in adolescence by using a variety of stage directions, dressings, and props.

Tricks of the trade include: directing girls to suck their fingers, lie in the fetal position, pout like a child, sleep with praying hands under their heads, shave their genitals, and grab both feet—like a baby—and pull back toward their heads; donning the girls in bobby socks, Mary Jane shoes, diapers,

pigtails, braces, ruffled shirts and socks, hair bows and bar-
rettes, oversized shoes, and distinctively adolescent shorts and
dresses; propping the set with dolls, rabbits, teddy bears, swing
sets, oversized chairs, Mickey Mouse phones, glasses of milk,
and schoolbooks.

Hustler also employs titles that indicate a child sex theme,
such as "Lolita," "Back To School," "Cynthia," "Baby Face,"
and "The Farmer's Daughter."

Playboy even ran an article, "Father Knows Best," a true-
life story of a photographer who photographed nude shots of
his daughter from youth to adulthood. *Playboy* ran select photos of the naked child. As one critic asked, "How will this
article affect other fathers who have a camera and young
daughters in the house?"

And there are other "adult" pornography magazines that
promote child sex. *Swank,* for example, advertises a blow-up
doll called, "Lolita Teenage Playmate."

Obviously, then, the "adult" pornography industry promotes children as sexual objects—which some believe induces
child sexual abuse.

Producing Pedophiles

Dr. Judith A. Reisman, who authored the study of *Playboy,*
Penthouse, and *Hustler* magazines and how these erotic publications promote child sexual abuse, explained how the material
creates child molesters. Dr. Reisman, who conducted the study
under a grant from the U.S. Department of Justice, said the
sexual stimulation of viewing naked children in magazines—
even if the pictorials are actually adults dressed as pseudo-
children—has a cumulative effect that, over a period of time,
heightens arousal for real children. Saying the mind cannot
disassociate in the brain between photographs and real children, Dr. Reisman believes the cumulative effect of these pornographic pictures is to create adults who lust after and sexually abuse children.

Dr. Reisman also likes to quote child psychiatrist Marianne Wamboldt and child pyschologist Janet Negley who say child sex photographs in "adult" pornography may make the pedophile less inhibited about his sexual feelings.

In a joint statement, they say, "Repeated exposure to sexual scenes with adolescent (or younger) girls could stimulate hidden sexual feelings towards young girls which the man had been keeping at bay.

"There is also an inherent permission given to indulge in this kind of sexual behavior when viewed in the media. Of particular concern is the relationship of step-parent to step-child, particularly stepfathers and stepdaughters. These pairs do not share a long history of nurturance; often a stepfather first meets his prospective stepdaughter as she is entering puberty. . . . Without a history to help suppress sexual feelings, these pairs often must consciously do so. To have media present scenes of child seduction may make it more difficult for men to consciously suppress these feelings."[14]

The sexual revolution, then, has given great impetus to the child sex molester.

Rummaging Through the Trash

The pedophile is like a scavenger. He searches through the garbage trying to find suitable trash to justify his existence. His efforts have not been in vain. Trash Pile One: A "new morality" that says sex between consenting partners is acceptable. Trash Pile Two: Popular culture that depicts children as sexually attractive, indiscriminate, energetic, and licentious. Trash Pile Three: Euphemisms—like "making love," and "sexual preference"—that are designed to protect homosexual and promiscuous sex. Trash Pile Four: "Adult" pornography that portrays children as objects of adult sexual desire.

Is it any wonder the pedophile feels he has a right to organize and practice his sexual perversion?

Society's obsession with wanton and "free sex" has netted

great social consequences—venereal diseases, broken homes, unwanted pregnancies, warped personalities, auto-erotic deaths, social expenditures to combat these ills, and now the raping of the nation's children.

The mainstream of society, of course, will deny these consequences. And it will continue to search for pills to cure venereal diseases, rid unwanted pregnancies, heal personality disorders, and reduce sexual drives of child molesters.

But the only real medicine society needs is to get off the slippery slope and back onto the foundation of God's truths.

Wayward Genes or Sin Nature?

What creates a child molester? No one knows. Some doctors will blame wayward genes and "learned behavior." More likely, however, child sexual abuse is sparked from no greater force than that which has prompted other crimes against humanity: Sin.

But it should not be surprising that society rejects this simple explanation. Eighty-four percent of the nation believes that human nature is fundamentally good![15] Yet, the Scriptures say, "There is none righteous, not even one; . . . Their throat is an open grave, with their tongues they keep deceiving, the poison of asps is under their lips; whose mouth is full of cursing and bitterness; their feet are swift to shed blood, destruction and misery are in their paths, and the path of peace have they not known, there is no fear of God before their eyes" (Rom. 3:10-18, NAS). If the Scriptures are correct (and they are) is it any surprise that child sexual abuse has increased as society tolerates more deviant sexual behavior and flaunts children as sexual objects? Of course not.

Sin, as any Christian knows, manifests itself in many forms—from bitterness to slander, strife to murder, covetousness to thievery, adultery to homosexuality, and drunkenness to drug abuse. The manifestations of sin are boundless, varying in intensity and degree, unpredictable, and timeless. The sin of child molesting is no different: it knows no boundaries, the molester may fondle the child or kill him in a violent rage; it varies in intensity and degree, the molester may have superior self-control over his lust for children or none at all; it is unpredictable, the molester may surface in a large city or a small town, in a family of means or a family of need, in a respected job profession or a job of low esteem; and it is timeless, the molester is not a product of the twentieth century. Like any sin, child sexual abuse spreads more rapidly as society provides the molester with greater enticement, acceptance, opportunity, excuses, and stimulation.

We know that 80 percent of all child molesters were abused themselves as children, that society provides the pedophile with a rational argument for having sex with children, that society accepts abnormal sex, that popular culture portrays children as hankering for promiscuous sex, that "adult" pornography promotes the sexual attractiveness of children, and that some social thinkers prefer to make excuses for the molester by blaming child sexual abuse on wayward genes and uncontrolled "learned behavior."

If these forces are combined, we can understand that they serve as a catalyst to the sin of child sexual abuse. And if these forces continue, society can only expect an increase in child sex offenders.

The Me Generation
It takes two to play.

Though child sex offenders feel they have a social right to exist and practice their perversion, this does not explain why pedophiles are so successful in finding children to molest.

Part of the reason has already been discussed: the pedophile uses his intelligence, authority, knowledge of child psychology, and organizational skills to apply peer pressure, affection, "good times," intimidation, friendship, attention, and security to persuade the child to have sex. That these strategies work is beyond dispute. But why do they work? If the child is receiving the warmth, love, attention and care he needs at home, why should he look elsewhere? The fact is, child sexual abuse has increased because many children are not receiving these basic childhood needs at home. And as a result, they become children psychologically primed for the molester. As Meredith S. stated, "I looked for the kid who didn't have a real good home life—the kid with the devil-may-care attitude." For these children are willing to sell their bodies as the price for basic human needs.

But why are so many children coming from poor home lives? There are several reasons. Social, economical, geographical, ancestral, racial, and philosophical forces can all contribute to wretched home lives. But the impact of most of these forces has generally improved during the twentieth century. That is, with the exception of one: philosophical.

Philosophically, individual family members are not as strongly committed to one another as in earlier years—say, just two decades ago. And the deterioration of this togetherness is reflected in increased broken homes, child runaways, drug and alcohol abuse among teenagers, suicides among adolescents, and child sexual abuse, to name a few consequences.

What was the social upheaval responsible for this breakdown in the family? A philosophical belief among many families that happiness, money, self-fulfillment, freedom, and future state were more important than husband, wife, or child. The social acceptance of this philosophy became undeniably evident during the 1970s.

The 1970s was a decade of narcissism—people had (and still possess) an unashamed admiration and fascination for their own self-interests. Nothing—absolutely nothing—should stand in the way of "Number One"—that is, Self. Neither morality, nor tradition, nor family, nor the opinion of others is to interfere with one's own happiness, fulfillment, objectives, or destiny.

The 1970s became the decade of the so-called Me Generation.

Looking Out for Number One. . . .

Explained Robert J. Ringer, author of *Looking Out For #1*, which is perhaps the bible of the Me Generation, "Morality—the quality of character—is a very personal and private matter. No other living person has the right to decide what is moral (right or wrong) for you. I further suggest that you make a prompt and thorough effort to eliminate from your life all individuals who claim—by words or actions, directly or by inference—to possess such a right. You should concern yourself only with whether looking out for Number One is moral from your own rational, aware viewpoint."[16]

Having dispensed with traditional morality, beliefs, and customs, Mr. Ringer leaves society with one primary criterion when making a decision: does it benefit Number One? If it benefits self, then the decision is moral.

It is not difficult to predict the tragic results a society will suffer when it puts the interests of *self* before the interests of others—especially before the interests of wife, husband, and children.

Yet, even in a family relationship the interests of Number One reign.

Explained Mr. Ringer, "A crummy love relationship is one in which you consistently give more than you receive. If you're in that predicament now, cut it off before it goes any further. Just because you've invested a number of valuable years in a relationship which has caused you more pain than pleasure, that doesn't mean you should throw away additional years enduring more of the same. . . . No reason is sound enough to keep a crummy relationship together. The worst excuse of all is children. If kids are involved, give them a break. Get out of your mate's life so your children can enjoy both of you at your best—in happier states than they now see you."[17]

"No matter how good the good," Mr. Ringer advises, "if the bad outweighs it, it's a crummy relationship. Staying in it can only be a fatal blow to looking out for Number One."[18]

And Forgetting the Kids

Though not every divorce, of course, is attributable to this philosophical outlook, it is interesting to note that during the years 1968-1980—the very years this nation saw a steady increase in child sexual abuse—the average married couple with children stayed together less than seven years! Could it be that these small children, growing up in a single-family home where the mother or father becomes the primary breadwinner, are looking elsewhere for love, friendship, and attention? The speculation is inescapable.

But divorce is only one problem the Me Generation has created for children. Others include parents who are so ambitious for money, prestige, careers, and pleasures that they neglect the needs of their children. These children (and I'm not being overly facetious) are often farmed off to day-care centers during the day, baby-sitters at night, and the streets, television sets, and video arcades in between.

As one historian described the current mindset of many parents, "Parents . . . increasingly seem to want to arrange their lives so that their children are minimally demanding and bothersome."[19]

With parents getting a divorce, forming new families, and placing children in day-care, many social thinkers have begun to ask, "Who's raising our children?"—a question that would seem absurd just twenty years ago.

The startling answer, as stated by Richard Ruopp, president of the Bank Street College of Education in New York, is, "We don't know who is raising our children."[20]

The facts: twenty million mothers with children under eighteen work[21] (and nearly 60 percent of women with children three to five years are working[22]); 5.7 million children receive care in day-care centers or neighborhood day-care homes[23]; since 1950, mothers in the work force have tripled[24]; only 24 percent(!) of women between the ages of eighteen and twenty-nine believe in the traditional family—husband assuming the primary role of breadwinner and the wife caring for home and child[25]; nearly 1,300 new stepfamilies with children under eighteen are forming *every day*[26]; 23 percent of all households are headed by a single parent[27]; in 1970 day-care centers barely existed, by 1982 there were 30,750 places whose principal receipts came from providing child care[28]; since 1970, the number of single parent homes has jumped 102 percent (almost seven million families)[29]; approximately 12.5 million children live with their mothers alone (or one in every five children!)[30]; and one-half of all single women have a child at home, and 21 percent have three or more children.[31]

If the child molester is on the hunt for the beleaguered child, the nation offers millions of vulnerable children from which to choose.

This is not to imply that every child—or that most children—in a day-care center, a step-family, or a single-family home is vulnerable. Neither does it imply that only children from these environments are vulnerable. The vulnerable child, quite frankly, is any child who is neglected because the parent pursues self-interests at the expense of the child.

Prime Candidates for Abuse

Those families that break apart because—as Mr. Ringer states—a parent has to give more than he or she receives are prime candidates for rearing vulnerable children. The Census Bureau reports that the median income of a single-parent family headed by a woman (approximately six million families) is a meager $9,000 a year.[32] These parents are always under pressure and pressed for time with no money to spend on timesaving devices. Furthermore, better than one in every three of these children will suffer depression and displacement. They encounter chronic and pronounced unhappiness, sexual promiscuity, delinquency in the form of drug and alcohol abuse, petty stealing, acts of breaking and entering, poor learning, intense anger, apathy, restlessness, and a sense of intense neediness.[33] And those single parents that later marry do not necessarily provide a better environment for their child. The Stepfamily Association of America states that such children are upset and depressed over the loss of their biological parent and are faced with a clash of values, traditions, and forced affection as they endure the enormous pressure of trying to fit into a new relationship.[34] Are these children vulnerable to the child molester who spends the greater part of his life searching for children who can respond to his overtures of affection, "good times," intimidation, friendship, attention, and security?

Families that neglect the needs of their children because they would rather spend their time pursuing careers, money, pleasures, and prestige are also prime candidates for rearing vulnerable children. Parents who brush their children aside—whether the reason is they have no interest in their children, or they view them as bothersome, or they would rather be drinking with friends, gambling at the racetrack, or watching television undisturbed—are also rearing vulnerable children.

According to the Education Commission of the States, there are at least two million children "at risk." These children, the Commission states, are alienated, unmotivated, lacking self-esteem, and *lacking family support.*[35]

In other words, the child molester has at least two million children spanning the nation that are prime subjects for sexual abuse. Is it any wonder, then, that child molester Ricky Lee G. can find more than 150 children in a small southern town to sexually abuse and then claim, "It's as natural as going to the refrigerator door and getting food out"?

It is highly unlikely then—either from the testimony of child molesters or from the conviction of common sense—that children from poor home environments are anything but children vulnerable to abuse.

The vulnerable child—and this merits repeating—is any child who comes from a family where the parent must neglect—or chooses to neglect—the needs of his or her child to pursue self-interests—whatever those interests may be.

The Devalued Child

The Me Generation is responsible for an overall devaluation of children.

Feminism told mothers to abandon child-rearing in favor of career opportunities. Pro-abortion advocates told mothers to kill their fetal child in favor of self-interests. State governments devalued the importance of children by passing easy "no fault" divorce laws. Public schools told parents that parenting should not be a primary concern because the schools would provide teachings on sexuality, values formation, death and dying, and decision-making skills. Population control advocates told society that a surplus of children will wreak havoc, or possibly destruction, on the world's natural resources. The federal government told mothers that children can be so excessively burdensome that the taxpayers will provide free contraceptives to needy women. Sociologists told parents the cost of children is so prohibitive that to have more than two would be an act of great social irresponsibility. And moral philosophers told families that self-fulfillment is of greater value than making personal sacrifices for children.

Several striking statistics provide persuasive arguments that the value of the child to parent has decreased during the past fifteen years.

The United States Census Bureau reported that fifty years ago only 19 percent of women aged twenty-five to twenty-nine years old were childless. Today nearly twice that amount, 37 percent, do not have children.[36]

In 1962, 84 percent of families surveyed believed all married couples who can ought to have children. Today, just 43 percent of those families believe married couples should have children.[37]

Finally, the median duration of a marriage with children is 6.9 years, while the median duration of a childless marriage is 4.2 years.[38] Therefore a child is a marital glue worth about three years!

The increase in child sexual abuse, then, is largely the product of the sexual revolution and the Me Generation. The sexual revolution gave the molester a social right to exist. The Me Generation gave the molester a host of vulnerable children primed for sexual abuse. Therefore, if the nation hopes to rid itself of this embarrassment, shame, and tragedy, it must return to traditional morals, values, and parenting.

EIGHT

FIGHTING BACK

Child sex abuse. How bad is it?

In a six-month period during 1985 (from March through September) people in the following job or youth volunteer positions across the nation were either indicted, convicted, or charged with child sexual abuse: a mayor, two high school principals, two school bus drivers, a state legislator, several ministers, five schoolteachers, a football coach, two day-care directors, two day-care teachers, five Boy Scout leaders, a baseball umpire, a girls' basketball coach, a city recreation department official, a gym teacher, two police officers, a school psychologist, president of a local Little League, a baseball team coach, and a church deacon. And this does not include people who were apprehended but do not work directly with children, such as the owner of a hair salon, a lawyer, a household product distributor, a marketing consultant, and sixteen men in Wichita, Kansas, who were arrested for operating a child prostitution ring. And, of course, this is *not* a comprehensive list.

How bad is child sexual abuse? It is bad enough that every parent should be aware that his or her child may be approached by a child predator—not once, but several times. And if that child is unprepared, or comes from a poor family environment, the odds of him being sexually molested are almost certain. If the reader remembers nothing else in this book, he should engrave in his mind the statement by Ricky Lee G. which tells the ease by which molesters abuse children, "It's as natural as going to the refrigerator door and getting food out." How much more natural if the child is psychologically primed for abuse.

So what needs to be done?

Much.

Society must adopt a new attitude toward child sex abuse. This means police agencies must develop better investigative and law enforcement procedures, the courts must stiffen their penalties against child molesters, legislators must pass laws that facilitate convictions and aid prevention of child sexual abuse, and government must provide financial and administrative support. Parents also must better care for and educate their children, and society must stop fostering a climate which allows pedophiles to breed and interact.

On the other hand, society must not engage in witch hunts, deny child molesters their legal rights, pass laws that unduly burden private agencies or innocent citizens, or excuse the child molester as being the victim of an "uncontrollable" sexual urge.

Raising Public Consciousness

With reports of child sexual abuse on every headline in every city, with television movies dramatizing the plight of abducted and abused children, and with homes having more pictures of missing children scattered around the house (on grocery bags, milk cartons, and pieces of mail) than pictures of their own children, it is fair to say the public is aware of child sexual abuse.

But is awareness enough? No.

The mother who packs her child off to school every day wants more than awareness that her child may be kidnapped and killed along the way. The father who drops his child off at the day-care center wants more than awareness that his child may be drugged and raped during the day. And the parent who allows his child to go unescorted to parks, video arcades, skating rinks, or public swimming pools wants more than awareness that the child may be the target of a pedophile.

More than awareness, the family wants solutions—a way to end child sexual abuse.

Unfortunately, society would like these solutions to be moderate, simple, easy, convenient, and—of course—instant; that is, the solutions should conveniently fit onto the back of an express mail postcard—and be hand delivered at that!

But real life doesn't work that way. In fact, the actual solutions require a great deal of effort, social change, commitment, hard work, study, and time.

Because the rapid spread of child sexual abuse did not occur in a day, it will not end in a nighttime. In fact, those evil forces—from a debasing of moral values to a plummeting of parental care—took decades of commingling before devastating the nation. Therefore, there is no overnight solution.

If society is to successfully stem the tide against this perverted sex, then society *must* begin by raising its level of moral fortitude and parental duty. Meanwhile, until traditional values and practices are restored, society must rely upon its reflexes and develop laws, programs, and policies that ferret out pedophiles, that protect our children, and that aid the conviction and punishment of child molesters. But these short-term actions must not be a substitute for the ultimate solution to child sexual abuse: a return to moral living.

For the most part, society remains ignorant about how to end child sexual abuse. Therefore, the public's consciousness must be raised until society fully understands the strategies that can bring an end to the raping of our children.

Law Enforcement

It would be both impractical and impossible to note everything law enforcement officials are doing to counter child sexual abuse. However, there are certain general trends that are worth noting.

Foremost, the law enforcement community has finally responded to the growing number of complaints by experts that it do more to eradicate the problem. Only a few years ago, the Northern California Juvenile Officers Association criticized police agencies as generally doing nothing about child molesters. Now many law enforcement agencies have trained their officers to handle child sex abuse complaints, and many have even formed special task forces to investigate and apprehend child molesters. These investigative strategies include canvassing playgrounds, video arcades, parks, and other typical pedophile hangouts. Police officers often question children about whether they have been approached by suspicious men or women. Surveillance equipment is often employed to keep a watchful eye on certain pedophilia hunting grounds. And police departments are using undercover agents to infiltrate pedophile groups.

These task forces also respond quickly to anonymous tips of possible pedophilia activity in a neighborhood. In fact, these anonymous tips are the foremost reason pedophiles are arrested in New York City.

Said Sgt. Samuel Alberti, who heads Manhattan's pedophilia unit, "The typical situation leading to an arrest is an anonymous call saying, 'Look, I live in such and such a place, and I know this guy down the hall. He constantly has twelve- and thirteen-year-old children going into his apartment, usually on a Friday and a Saturday night. There's an awful lot of noise going on—parties, and kids, so on and so on.' And we surmise that this is a pedophile. So we begin an investigation. We set up surveillance. We canvass the area. And we continue to probe this fellow until we determine whether he is molesting children."[1]

Prior to the establishment of these task forces, police agencies not only failed to organize any effort to ferret out pedophiles, but child sex abuse crimes routinely fell into the hands of amateur officers. Unlike procedures followed on most crimes, child sex abuse cases were not handled by a "specialist system;" that is, initial investigation by a police officer was not followed up by a person who specializes in child sexual abuse crimes. Without this expertise or experience, police agencies failed to both prevent sex crimes or apprehend pedophiles. But with the establishment of task forces, police agencies have made measurable gains against child sexual abuse.

The FBI

The Federal Bureau of Investigation has also stepped up measures to apprehend child molesters. But because it is a federal agency, the FBI's involvement is somewhat restricted. It can only become involved in child sex abuse cases when the pedophile violates a federal law, such as when the pedophile kidnaps a child or becomes involved in the interstate transportation of child pornography.

Nevertheless, the FBI has sought ways to strengthen its investigation into sexual molestation cases. In the spring of 1983, the FBI formed its first child sex abuse task force. Operating in New York City, the task force has had three objectives: (1) to determine whether the abductor is sexually involved with the child, (2) to determine whether abducted children are being used as prostitutes, and (3) to determine whether abducted children are being used in pornography.

Explained Lee Laster, director of the force, "We created it out of an overall concern about the sexual exploitation of kids. Are they involved in pornography? Are they involved in child prostitution? Are they involved with molesters? Are they being kidnapped to be sold? And how many murdered children were killed due to sexual exploitation?

"Along the way, of course, we want to put people in jail."[2]

Many police agencies, however, would like the FBI to do more, such as become a central power from which the local police could operate. Due to the mobility of the pedophile (he can abduct a child in one state and swiftly flee to another, or be convicted in one state and relocate in another), police officials encounter many jurisdictional problems while trying to quickly apprehend the molester. A police department in Jackson, Mississippi, for instance, would have great difficulty learning that a pedophile either fled to or came from Winston-Salem, North Carolina, since there is no central communication power linking all the police departments together. There is the additional problem of police in one jurisdiction having no legal authority in another. Although a police department would certainly attempt to locate a child molester that may have fled to its jurisdiction, it would usually not give the matter higher priority than its own investigations. Besides, how many police departments would need to be notified that a child molester may be fleeing to their jurisdiction? Conceivably, the molester could choose any one of thousands to make his new home. This problem, then, provides the molester with a great opportunity to flee quickly to another city, county, or state. A possible solution to this problem, if the FBI acted as a central power, would be to establish a national computer that allowed police departments to log in the details of the abductor and abduction. Then, if any police department in another jurisdiction picked up a suspect for whatever reasons, it could easily check the suspect's description against those filed in the national computer.

The FBI is already using a version of this recommendation to locate missing children. The FBI's National Crime Information Center computer allows police to enter information about missing children immediately onto the national computer which then becomes available to law enforcement agencies across the county.

U.S. Customs
Though both the FBI and local police have greatly increased their investigative strategies against the child molester, no law

enforcement agency, *as a whole*, has done more to ferret out the pedophile than U.S. Customs.

This is true because Customs Commissioner William Von Raab has made it a priority in his agency to stop the illegal importation of pornographic books, magazines, films, and video tapes. In 1983, his agency netted a 120 percent increase in pornography seizures over 1982; and seizures in 1984 doubled those of 1983. Of the 4,266 pornography seizures in 1984, more than one-half involved children.[3]

Commissioner Von Raab initiated the agency's vigorous enforcement of obscenity laws because he believed the "nation's moral health was at stake."[4] In fact, when he took office under the Reagan Administration, he sent a letter to all his employees stressing his "personal concern about the influence pornography is having on our country. I want all my employees, indeed all the nation, to be outraged by this trash and join our struggle to eliminate it."[5]

Within twenty months, Von Raab's child pronography crackdown led to the arrest of numerous child pornographers, recipients, pedophiles, and child molesters. These arrests included teachers, family counselors, clergy, and medical personnel.

The crackdown was so successful that customs officers in the field were reporting, nearly every day, new cases of seizures and arrests of pornography recipients.

Special Agent Walter O'Mally, who operates out of the agency's Chicago branch, explained the strategy which U.S. Customs follows to seize pornography and apprehend pedophiles.[6]

Since the majority (85 percent) of all child pornography is imported from the Netherlands, Sweden, and Denmark, U.S. Customs periodically screens packages arriving to the United States from these source countries.

This task, as can be imagined, is extremely difficult. And even after watching mail specialists adroitly pore over and magically isolate child pornography, it is somewhat impossible to comprehend. For not only is every piece of mail arriving from a source country examined, but the parcel itself is camouflaged in any one of a number of disguises. As can be expected, the parcel never arrives in a brown, magazine-size envelope, with a return address marked, *Lolita* magazine. Instead, child pornography is typically disguised in a business or letter-size envelope with such bogus return addresses as Japan Air Lines, Nordic Auto, Dutch Travel Service, or Antiquarian Books. Some child pornography magazines are wrapped in rolled newspapers, or stuffed in envelopes that are highlighted with drawings of children and flowers on its cover. How the mail specialist locates one of these concealed packages is an instinct even the customs inspector cannot explain.

But once one package is located, the bogus return address becomes a red flag for all other packages attempting the same subterfuge. And of course, once the package is identified, the addresses of all pedophiles receiving the same pornography item are also identified.

As Agent O'Mally stated, "We have potential child abusers delivered to our doorsteps every day."

Receiving a child pornography package, however, does not mean the recipient is a pedophile. Perhaps the recipient was the butt of a sick joke, received it by mistake, or from a vindictive enemy. At any rate, few judges would be willing to issue an arrest or search warrant based on one obscene parcel. So Customs develops an index file on the recipient and logs each child pornography seizure which it confiscates going to that same address.

Meanwhile, Customs officials investigate the recipient's background, primarily to determine whether the individual has a child abuse history, small children at home, a job involving children, or membership in any pedophilia organization. Also, while Customs gathers its evidence, the Post Office may attempt a "sting operation" against the suspected pedophile. This so-called "sting operation" involves a postal official, posing as a fellow pedophile, writing the suspect a letter in an attempt to get the individual to admit being a child molester. The letter may ask the suspect for a meeting to swap child pornography pictures, or to write about a personal sexual experience with a child, or to acknowledge any act that would be an admission of child sexual abuse.

If investigations at Customs reveal the suspect is a pedophile, it then presents its evidence—multiple child pornography seizures, previous arrest records, his response to the Post Office's "sting operation" —to attorneys at the Justice Department. And if the attorneys agree there is probable cause to investigate further, Customs initiates what it calls a "controlled delivery."

Put simply, a "controlled delivery" means Customs reintroduces a previously seized child pornography parcel back into the mail stream.

The suspect's home is then surrounded with surveillance equipment. Once the recipient takes the package from his mailbox and into the home, his residence is searched for the "controlled" package and any other child pornography items that may be found.

In 1984 alone, Customs used this and other procedures to apprehend over twenty pedophiles nationwide.[7]

Law Enforcement Handicaps

Though law enforcement officials have made great gains in investigating and arresting child molesters, there are still many handicaps to overcome.

Many local police departments are still without resources, manpower, and expertise to handle child sex abuse cases; it still takes an average of one and a half years to effect just one arrest; children (and their parents) are very frequently uncooperative with investigations; porn distributors hide behind a myriad of "fly by night" dummy corporations, making them almost impossible to track; legal jurisdictions all too frequently interfere with child abuse investigations; pedophilia groups are very difficult to infiltrate since undercover policemen find it hard to portray themselves as the people they are investigating; and many law enforcement officials have become discouraged because the courts, in general, give probation or light sentences to convicted pedophiles.

Society, however, can take heart that law enforcement officials have stepped up measures to prevent child abuse and apprehend child molesters. Granted, more can be done. And with enough public pressure, more will be done. Obviously, however, law enforcement alone will not end child sexual abuse, and this the parent must never forget. Even as law enforcement does not end drug abuse, or robbery, or even traffic violations, child sexual abuse will not be stopped even by the most vigorous, dedicated, professional, or united police action.

In order for child sexual abuse to end, parents must return to parenting, and society must return to traditional moral standards. If not, the heart of the pedophile will continue to find roots in today's sexual revolution, and children will continue to try to find the love and affection that truly is a biological need.

Government Action

As can be expected, child sexual abuse has prompted cries from all social quarters demanding that government do something, which—as usual—means government should spend more money and pass more laws.

More money is needed, and it is not necessary to belabor the point here. Suffice it to say, money is needed to provide equipment and staff for apprehending child molesters, locating missing children, and interviewing, diagnosing, and treating abused children. Child abuse centers frequently complain of lack of funds to accept new cases, to hire secretaries or hire security guards, to handle media inquiries, or even to buy file cabinets. How much money federal, state, or local governments should provide is beyond the scope of this book. But common sense dictates that the government should not allow more children to become abused because fiscal conservatives are concerned about budget excesses.

Good Laws, Bad Laws
Government should also pass laws. But here a line must be drawn. Laws should facilitate the prevention, conviction, and deterrence of child sex abuse *without* abusing the rights of others.

An example of such a law was a child pornography statute passed in Congress during the spring of 1984. The law increased fines for distributing child pornography by ten times, it no longer required prosecutors to prove the photographs were obscene, and it raised the age of victims from sixteen to eighteen years old. This last amendment was very important to prosecutors for, under the old law, it was very difficult to prove that, say, a girl who looked fourteen years old was not actually sixteen. But, under the new law, prosecutors can easily prove that a young-looking girl is not eighteen years old.

Some other examples of laws that should be pursued include:

- Criminal background checks on people who teach, train, or care for children. The law should be reasonable, however, and not subject people to criminal review if their time spent with children is only minimal—such as baby-sitting or teaching Sunday School. Furthermore, the law should not prohibit people from working with children simply because they have been accused, rather than convicted, of a crime—as some would prefer.

- Mandatory punishments for convicted child molesters, and laws that prohibit courts from giving probation and suspended sentences to repeated offenders.

- Prohibition on the use of computers to log sexual information about children and to transmit that information to fellow pedophiles. Currently, no federal law prohibits such communications.

- Permission to allow children to testify in court via live two-way closed-circuit television. This is different than videotaped testimony, for it allows the accused child molester to see his accuser and for his defense attorney to question the child's testimony.

- Proposals requiring school officials to telephone parents when their children are absent from school.

Samples of laws that should not be pursued include:

- Greater regulation of day-care centers. This "Big Daddy" approach will do nothing to prevent children from being sexually abused. In fact, most of the day-care centers charged with child sexual abuse are already licensed and regulated. This is true because regulations are easily circumvented. The "Big Daddy" approach not only supplants the duty of the parent (who is ultimately responsible for selecting a safe day-care environment), but it violates the rights of people operating these day-care centers by assuming they are guilty and by forcing them to prove their innocence through the adoption of expensive state and federal regulations. Furthermore, regulations hardly carry the moral force necessary to prevent an extremely demented person from sexually abusing children.

- Criminal penalties for failing to report suspected cases of child sexual abuse. According to this incredulous plan, people could be sent to jail for failing to notify authorities of possible sex abuse cases. Every citizen, of course, has a moral and legal duty to report a crime. But the above legislation goes beyond this. It requires individuals to report even suspected crimes, or go to jail. Such legislation is barbaric, without legal precedent, and lacking sound mind.

- Permit videotaped or "hearsay" testimony. This type of legislation is a total affront to the U.S. Constitution. Regardless of the hideous nature of the crime, every suspected criminal—even a suspected child abuser—has a constitutional right to face his accuser. But the aforementioned legislation would allow a child's testimony to be presented on a pre-recorded videotape, or through a third-party, such as allowing therapists, teachers, or child counselors to speak for the child. Considering children frequently lie about being abused, this type of legislation is both unjust and morally repugnant.

The above-mentioned legislations, of course, do not represent a comprehensive list of bills that have been considered or passed by the various legislatures. (This would be an impossible task. New York alone debated forty-three child sex abuse bills during 1985, and California debated over a hundred!) However, the selected legislations do illustrate the difference between practical solutions to child sexual abuse, and those that trample on rights, privacies, and human dignity in a haphazard attempt to fight child abuse.

In the upcoming days, many more laws will be introduced, debated, and passed in an effort to turn the tide against child sexual abuse. But as society wrangles over these bills, it must never forsake the scales of justice. Each law should be designed to facilitate the prevention, conviction, and deterrence of child sexual abuse without violating the rights, privileges, privacies, or honor of any citizen.

Public Schools Educating Children

Another area of active involvement by the government is the use of public schools to educate children about child sexual abuse.

Though programs vary from school district to school district, such education is usually presented in the form of a play. Performed by adults, the typical skit tells the story of a child who is confused about whether his step-father's hugs, kisses, and touches are an act of affection or sexual abuse. When the child is assured that the step-father is making sexual advances, he is persuaded to tell an adult. Once the play is over, the schoolchildren are told that they too should report similar cases of sexual assault. The children are then invited to come forward and tell the actors their personal nightmares.

Such education is beneficial for two reasons: (1) parents generally feel ill-equipped about such matters and are reluctant to teach their children; and (2) some parents are the very ones abusing the children and, therefore, have no interest in teaching the child about sexual abuse.

Regardless of these benefits, however, the public schools are not the place to teach children about sexual abuse. Considering the immaturity of these young minds, it is much too easy for the child to misinterpret the purpose of these plays. The child may come away believing step-fathers are evil, that homes are dangerous, or that child sexual abuse is any prolonged hug, bounce on the knee, or tickle under the rib cage. In fact, many parents, relatives, and friends of the family have been falsely accused through such programs.

The ideal place to teach children about sexual abuse is at home or church.

But if parents continue to neglect this responsibility, and child sexual abuse statistics continue to rise, then the public schools will continue to usurp this parental duty—even though such educational programs can drive deep wedges into family bonds.

The Courts

When police raided David F.'s home on the south side of Chicago, they stumbled into the type of mire that even the swine avoid. Not only did they find fifty kiddie porn magazines, a large selection of pedophile books, and 8mm films of children having sex with adults, but they discovered photos of children whom he molested. And not only did these photos depict the children being violated by pens, pencils, toothbrushes, hot dogs, and dildos, but he actually kept most of these soiled items in a metal box as a remembrance.

Also in David F.'s collection were clippings of girls' underwear from a Sears magazine; soiled panties which he gave the girls and later demanded they return; catalogs depicting women having sex with chickens, cows, dogs, and eels; and an order form for sound recordings of pain being inflicted on a person through spanking, bondage, and discipline—sound "so realistic that you can almost feel the sting of the lash biting into your own flesh," the advertisement reads. One book, appropriately called *Perversions,* actually showed two lesbians having sex in a coffin. And, though hardly conceivable at this point, David F. still had other sexual paraphernalia that cannot be described in this book.

So perverted was David F. that he even had a medical journal called *The Diseases of Children,* which contained still photos of naked children carrying the most dreadful diseases. And in his personal photo collection, David F. actually had a photo—which he took—of a badly burned girl sitting naked in his bathtub.

This case was not presented to sicken the reader or to indulge in descriptive excesses, but to fully prepare the reader to understand the shocking court decision that followed. David F., who pled guilty to two felony counts, was sentenced to only five years *probation* and pyschiatric counseling—the man never spent a day in jail! Even more appalling, the court agreed to allow David F. to marry a woman with three children—two of whom were minors!

This type of court decision is typical. Many convicted child molesters are given probated sentences—sometimes even after repeated arrests—before being sentenced to jail. And even then their jail sentence is only for a few years. And, if convicted yet again, it is not untypical for the court to sentence the molester to only a few years longer than his first prison term.[8]

A Need for Justice

The nation's courts are rife with rulings that stagger the imagination. In San Antonio, a child molester had a nineteen-year history of sexually abusing children before the court sentenced him to prison.[9] In Alexander, Virginia, a federal judge made the bold move to apologize for "not giving any jail sentence" to a previously convicted child pornography distributor but then made the amazing decision to only sentence the man to ninety days in jail upon his second conviction.[10]

In Montgomery County, Maryland, a circuit court sentenced a man to five years of psychiatric counseling for sexually abusing a seven-year-old child, even though the man refused to admit his guilt of committing the crime.[11] In Trenton, N.J., the state appeals court shaved off thirty-nine years of a sixty-three-year sentence of a man convicted of raping a child. The appellate court said the sentence was "clearly unreasonable."[12]

And in Norwood, Ohio, a county judge sentenced two men to only three months in jail for having sex with an eight-year-old girl. Judge Gilbert Bettman justified his lenient sentence saying the sexual incidents were "consensual." He added, "There are two misunderstandings. One, that the law can change everything, and it can't; and that the penitentiary is the answer to all society's problems, which it isn't."[14]

Though people committing crimes against children are prosecuted and convicted more often than any other criminal, they receive shorter sentences. In fact, according to a U.S. Justice Department study, only 13 percent of those convicted of sexually assaulting children receive a prison sentence of more than a year—less than two out of ten child molesters![13]

Why are the courts so lenient? There are several explanations: (1) Most courts believe that since child sexual abuse is a nonviolent crime—meaning the child was not physically battered—the molester should not be severely punished, especially if the molester is an outstanding citizen in every other manner. (2) Some believe the child molester will change his behavior after being caught, reprimanded, and given some pyschiatric counseling. (3) Some actually blame the children for instigating the crime. (4) Still others claim the prisons are already too crowded.

But with the explosion of child sexual abuse cases, the courts have begun to issue stiffer prison sentences. Yet even here, the courts are well below what justice would seem to dictate. Prison terms typically range from three to ten years upon first conviction which, though preferable to suspended sentences, is still inexcusable considering the average child molester, left untreated, will repeat his crime.

Treating the Molester

There are four major forms of treatment for child sex offenders: psychotherapy, behavior therapy, surgery, and medication.

Psychotherapy blames sexually deviant behavior on a person's unconscious internal conflicts. This treatment is supposed to cure the child molester by having the individual dig deep into his past in an attempt to discover what went wrong and when. If the molester understands what caused him to be a pedophile, this therapy holds, he can use this new insight to overcome his cravings for children. There is little evidence, however, that psychotherapy offers any more help to a child molester than, say, it would offer a chain-smoker who recalled what started him smoking.

Behavior therapy is the most disturbing treatment of all. It attempts to cure a child molester of his lust for children by teaching him to become sexually aroused at formerly non-arousing, but age-appropriate, partners. For instance, a common form of therapy is to send a mild electrical shock to the penis when photos of young children are flashed before the molester. At the same time, the molester is encouraged to masturbate while looking at nude, age-appropriate partners. Other forms of therapy include hypnosis and biofeedback. Though working well in the laboratory, these therapies fail miserably in non-laboratory settings.

Treatment through surgery includes nothing more than removing the testes. This operation is popularly known as castration which, contrary to popular myth, does not mean the penis is removed or that the man cannot have sex afterwards. Removal of the testes simply lowers testosterones which in turn lowers the intensity of erotic desire, but sex is still possible. The surgery has had good results but, for yet to be explained reasons, doctors seldom employ the operation—probably because the public, with its misconception of what the operation involves, views castration with a great sense of opprobrium.

The treatment now gaining most recognition and acceptance is a medication called Depo-Provera. In effect, Depo-Provera is a chemical castration. Injected once a week and gradually released into the bloodstream over several days, Depo-Provera chemically lowers testosterones which, as stated above, decreases the intensity of sexual cravings. When combined with group counseling—such as who to call, situations to avoid, and early warning signs—Depo-Provera can be very effective. At the Johns Hopkins University School of Medicine, Baltimore, Maryland, over 130 sexual deviants had been treated with Depo-Provera spanning a one-year period with a relapse rate of less than 5 percent.[15]

Though surgical and chemical castration offer hope for the child molester, such treatment should not become a substitute for punishing a convicted child molester—as some doctors and courts would argue.

Wayward Genes or Wayward Doctor?

Dr. Fred S. Berlin, an assistant professor at the Johns Hopkins Medical School, is a leading advocate for treating molesters in lieu of punishment.[16]

Believing pedophilia is a "learned" behavior which is oftentimes rooted in a born "biological" drive for children, Dr. Berlin argues that the child molester cannot possibly control his drive for children. The molester, this theory holds, is a victim of wayward genes.

"There is no reason to believe that it is any easier for the fixated homosexual pedophile to lose his interest in children and to become sexually aroused by females, than it would be for the average male to instead begin lusting for young boys," Dr. Berlin has stated.

Saying "People do not decide voluntarily what will arouse them sexually," Dr. Berlin contends that convicted child molesters should be medically treated, not sentenced to prison since "there is absolutely nothing about [incarceration] . . . that is going to have him come out of prison any less attracted to younger boys," he has written.

And Dr. Berlin holds no idle belief in his theory. He has asked judges on several occasions to impose Depo-Provera and psychiatric counseling on convicted child molesters in lieu of prison sentences.

In Montgomery County, Maryland, Dr. Berlin actually

succeeded in convincing a circuit court judge to impose a psychiatric and medical program in lieu of a prison term. He argued that to send convicted child molester Eric L. to prison for sexually abusing ten boys would be "punishing him for something he cannot control."

Judge James McAuliffe agreed. He said putting child molesters in prison, where they will be attacked by hardened criminals, "would be cruel and unusual punishment."

Eric L., a gymnastics instructor, had been previously convicted of sexually abusing children in 1972, 1975, and 1979 before his most recent arrest.

Justice Demands Punishment for the Convicted

This book will not attempt to set forth hard and fast rules for handing down prison sentences to convicted child molesters. But, taking a traditional approach to crime and punishment, justice demands that the convicted child molester be punished—not probated, not rehabilitated, not treated—but punished for his crime—a punishment sufficient to deter others from committing similar crimes, to serve justice to the abused child and his family, and to promote a sense of security among the public. The justice system must send a message that it will not tolerate child sexual abuse. But to continually excuse child molesters for their crime—whether the excuse be that the crime is non-violent or that treatment is preferable—is to promote social unrest and to increase the risk of more abused children. If child molesters learn that they will not be punished, but rather treated—through state-funded programs, at that!—these molesters will no longer have a deterrent for committing crimes against children. In fact, some may view the free medical treatment (in lieu of punishment) as a benefit of getting caught.

Though the issue needs to be publicly debated, the state should consider both stiff sentences and medical treatment for convicted child molesters.

Witch Hunts

Child sexual abuse lends itself easily to witch hunts because the crime has been explosive, uncontrollable, frightening, unpredictable, confusing, widespread, and emotionally volatile. And any time a social threat produces this many attacks on the public's sense of security, the risk of a witch hunt is inevitable.

And child sexual abuse is no different. Its share of casualties include teachers who have been falsely accused by disgruntled students, divorced husbands who have been falsely accused by non-custodial (as well as custodial) wives, fathers who have been falsely accused by a child's misinterpretation of affectionate feelings, day-care operators who have been falsely accused by imaginative and misled children, and parents who have been falsely accused by prosecutors who seem more anxious to achieve notoriety than the truth.

So, as the nation grapples with child sexual abuse, it is evident that another class of innocent victims are rising to the forefront—the falsely accused. In many cases, these guiltless victims of society's witch hunts may suffer greater harm than most abused children. Adults who are falsely accused may never recover. They may lose their reputation, job, children, and home. Or they may be forever held in suspicion, derision, and ostracism. And if the falsely accused fail to successfully defend their cases, they may even spend years in jail.

Keeping a Level Head

Society, therefore, must attack child sexual abuse through fair-minded actions. People should not be suspected of sexual abuse because they wink at children, offer them candy, or address them as "sweethearts." Nor should the motives of adults be questioned because they hug a child, offer to baby-sit, or volunteer for a youth organization. Such paranoia is both unwarranted and harmful. And, as this book has pointed out, the characteristics and strategies of a child molester are much more complex and obvious than these innocent gestures of good intentions. Besides, such hysteria and false accusations only feed the fire of suspicion which prompts more false accusations and mistrust of motives.

Furthermore, knowing that children and adults falsely accuse for malicious reasons or with honest intentions, society must take painstaking measures to ensure the civil and constitutional rights of each accused molester are protected. Prior to conviction, people should not be thrown into jail based simply on the testimony of a young child. Many children falsely accuse through misunderstanding or through the suggestive proddings of parents, prosecutors, brothers and sisters, social workers and counselors, and even other children. If evidence other than a child's testimony does not exist, a house arrest is sufficient.

The humiliation of being handcuffed in front of neighbors or thrown into jail with criminals based on an accusation of a single child is unconscionable.

Described one female day-care operator who was falsely accused of child sexual abuse and thrown in a Bronx, New York, jail overnight, "I've gone through hell. I've never been so humiliated. . . . I screamed that I didn't want to spend the night (in jail). . . . I don't want to remember that night. The roaches. The prostitutes. Even the matrons. They asked me how I liked—children. The prostitutes started yelling that they'd kill me if I was put in their cell. I sat all night on this hard, wood bench, roaches crawling all over. It smelled of urine and ammonia. It was the longest night in my life." The woman was even placed on a chain gang with prostitutes as she was led to a special grand jury which cleared her of charges that she fondled the genitals of three children.[17]

Granted, it is difficult for society to remain calm and rational while hundreds of children are being sexually abused almost daily. But it is for these very reasons—irrationality, over-anxiousness, and a quickness to point the accusatory finger—that our justice system must ensure that each accused molester receives a fair trial and be treated as innocent until proven guilty. Implied in this great American tradition, then, is that the child witness not be afforded the unfair advantage over the accused molester through the presentation of video-recorded testimony, hearsay evidence, or the refusal by the courts to allow the child to be cross-examined.

Unless this simple, historic, and just tradition is practiced, the witch hunters will not only falsely round up upstanding citizens, but they will hang them as well.

NOTES

Chapter 1: A Nation Alarmed

1. *Midland Reporter-Telegram,* 6 June, 1984.
   Claire Dawson-Brown, Testimony before the U.S. Senate Juvenile Justice Subcommittee, 8 August, 1984.

2. "Porno Ring in U.S. Cracked," *L.A. Times,* 8 May, 1982.
   "Mistrial in Child Pornography Case Declared," *L.A. Times,* 5 October, 1983.
   "Woman Charged in Child Pornography Operation," *N.Y. Times,* 1982.
   "Porn 'Queen' Pleads Guilty," *News and Daily Advance,* 15 February, 1984.
   "Los Angeles Pressing Inquiry Into Sexual Abuse of Children," *New York Times,* 1 April, 1984.
   News and Daily Advance, 23 July, 1984.

3. Seth L. Goldstein, "Investigating Child Sexual Exploitation: Law Enforcement's Role," *FBI Law Enforcement Bulletin,* January 1984, p. 26.

4. Goldstein, p. 26.

5. *St. Paul Sunday Pioneer Press,* 1 February, 1984.
   USA Today, 16 August, 1984.
   News and Daily Advance, 21 August, 1984.
   New York Times, 3 September, 1984.

New York Times, 6 September, 1984.

New York Times, 11 September, 1984.

New York Times, 21 September, 1984.

New York Times, 23 September, 1984.

Richmond Times Dispatch, 28 September, 1984.

USA Today, 16 October, 1984.

Richmond Times Dispatch, 17 October, 1984.

USA Today, 17 October, 1984.

Newsweek, 29 October, 1984.

New York Times, 21 November, 1984.

Washington Post, 21 November, 1984.

New York Daily News, 29 November, 1984.

Richmond Times Dispatch, 30 November, 1984.

New York Daily News, 19 January, 1985.

Washington Post, 2 January, 1985.

6. Kee MacFarlane, Testimony before the House Ways and Means Committee, Select Committee on Children, Youth, and Families, House of Representatives, 17 September, 1984.

7. Study conducted by Diana E. H. Russell, professor of sociology at Mills College, Oakland, California. Reported in *USA Today,* 7 August, 1984.

8. *Topeka Capital-Journal,* 17 September, 1983.

9. *USA Today,* 27 July, 1984.

10. *Fundamentalist Journal,* September 1984.

11. *New York Times,* 24 April, 1984.
New York Times, 2 October, 1984.
New York Times, 26 May, 1984.
New York Times, 9 September, 1984.
News and Daily Advance, 2 October, 1984.

12. *News and Daily Advance,* 9 December, 1984.

13. *Omaha World-Herald,* 22 February, 1984.
Sunday World-Herald, 19 February, 1984.
New York Times, 25 May, 1984.

14. Goldstein, p. 24, 28.

15. *Examiner,* 7 June, 1983.
Goldstein, p. 26.

16. *Washington Post,* 10 January, 1985.
    USA Today, 11 January, 1985.

17. *Washington Post,* 24 December, 1984.

18. *USA Today,* 5 December, 1984.

19. *Richmond Times Dispatch,* 27 June, 1984.

20. *Time,* 23 April, 1984.
    Newsweek, 14 April, 1984.

21. *USA Today,* 1 August, 1984.

Chapter 2: From the Gutter to the Streets

1. Toby Tyler and Lore E. Stone, Testimony before the Senate Permanent Subcommittee on Investigations, U.S. Senate, 19 November, 1984.

2. Vladimir Nabokov, *Lolita* (New York: G. P. Putnam's Sons, 1955).

3. *Lolita,* dir. Stanley Kubrick, based on *Lolita,* by Vladimir Nabokov, 1961.

4. Bosley Crowther, "Screen: 'Lolita'," *New York Times,* 14 June, 1962.

5. *Taxi Driver,* dir. Martin Scorsese, 1976.

6. *Pretty Baby,* dir. Louis Malle, 1977.

7. *Playboy,* January 1978.

8. *New York Times,* 3 April, 1981.

9. *New York Times,* 3 April, 1981.

10. John Camp, *St. Paul Sunday Pioneer Press,* 1 February, 1984.

11. *USA Today,* 27 December, 1984.

12. *USA Today,* 16 November, 1984.
    "A Sordid Game," *Newsweek,* 9 April, 1984.
    Richmond Times, 17 February, 1985.
    Washington Post, 28 September, 1984.

13. Nadine Brozan, "Light on Child Sex Abuse," *New York Times,* 30 April, 1984.

14. Robert O. Hook, U.S. Justice Department specialist on crimes committed against children.

15. Hook.

16. " 'Letter From a Pedophile,' " *Newsweek,* 14 May, 1984.

Chapter 3: Strategies of the Child Molester

1. *Newsweek,* 14 May, 1984.

2. *New York Daily News,* 13 August, 1984.

3. Lee Laster, interview with author, 7 March, 1984.

4. Ann W. Burgess, A. Nicholas Grath, and Maureen P. Causland, *American Journal Orthopsychiatric,* January, 1981.

5. Burgess, *American Journal Orthopsychiatric.*

6. Kenneth V. Lanning and Ann W. Burgess, "Child Pornography and Sex Rings," FBI *Law Enforcement Bulletin,* January, 1984.

7. Laster.

8. Kee MacFarlane, Testimony before the House Ways and Means Committee, Select Committee on Children, Youth, and Families, U.S. House of Representatives, 17 September, 1984.

9. Burgess, *American Journal Orthopsychiatric.*

10. Dr. Caroline Swift, Director of South West Community Health Center, Columbus, Ohio, in "Investigating Child Sexual Exploitation: Law Enforcement's Role," FBI *Law Enforcement Bulletin,* January, p. 25.

11. Lanning, pp. 12-13.

12. U.S. Customs Service paper summarizing current cases, August 1984.

13. *Lolita* 47.

14. *Nymph Lover.*

15. Seth Goldstein, "Investigating Child Sexual Exploitation: Law Enforcement's Role," FBI *Law Enforcement Bulletin,* January 1984, p. 26.

16. Goldstein, p. 26.

17. Goldstein, p. 26.

18. Toby Tyler and Lore E. Stone, Testimony before the Senate Permanent Subcommitte on Investigations, U.S. Senate, 19 November, 1984.

19. *Person to Person Directory* (Los Angeles, Calif., 1977)

20. *Person to Person Directory.*

21. *Person to Person Directory.*

22. *Person to Person Directory.*

23. *Lolita 13.*

24. *Lolita 50.*

25. *Lolita 50.*

26. *Lolita 50.*

27. *Lolita 31.*

28. *Lolita 31.*

29. *Lolita 31.*

30. *Lolita 47.*

31. *Lolita 50.*

32. "To be Young, Free *and* Admired," *Nudist Moppets* (Studio City, Calif.), Winter/Spring 1974.

33. *Richardson Report,* 29 July, 1983.
    Los Angeles Times, 27 August, 1983.

34. *San Jose Mercury News,* 10 April, 1984.
    Los Angeles Herald Examiner, 7 April, 1984.
    New York Times, 13 April, 1984.

35. Kee MacFarlane, Testimony before the House Ways and Means Committee, Select Committee on Children, Youth, and Families, U.S. House of Representatives, 17 September, 1984.

36. The following statements by Lee Laster were made to author on 7 March, 1984.

37. The following statements by Gary Hewitt were made to author on 8 March, 1984.

38. *New York Times,* 24 August, 1984.

39. The following statements by Gary Hewitt were made to author on 19 March, 1984.

40. Kenneth V. Lanning and Ann W. Burgess, "Child Pornography and Sex Rings," *FBI Law Enforcement Bulletin,* January 1984, p. 14.
    Ann Burgess, A. Nicholas Groth, and Maureen McCausland, *American Journal Orthopsychiatric,* January 1981.

New York Times, 6 May, 1984.

Newsweek, 14 May, 1984.

41. Lanning and Burgess, pp. 15-16.

42. Kenneth J. Herrman, Jr. and Michael John Jupp, Testimony before the Senate Permanent Subcommittee on Investigations, U.S. Senate, 29 November, 1984.

Chapter 7: The Forces Behind Child Sexual Abuse

1. Claire Chambers, *The SIECUS Circle,* Western Islands, Belmont, Mass., 1977, p. 19.

2. Chambers, p. 37.

3. Joseph Fletcher, *Humanhood: Essays in Biomedical Ethics,* Prometheus Books, 1975, p. 46.

4. Fletcher, p. 35.

5. Fletcher, p. 32.

6. Eike-Henner Kluge, *The Practice of Death,* Yale University Press, 1975, p. 228.

7. Kluge, p. 237.

8. Edward Brongersma, *Lolita 47.*

9. Peter Scales, *SIECUS Report,* Vol. VI, No. 4, March 1978.

10. U.S. Customs case no. PH07TE413509.

11. The following statements by Tish Ambrose, Al Goldstein, Marc Stevens, Gloria Leonard, Joyce Snyder, and Howard Farber were made to author during the week of May 13-17, 1985.

12. *Playboy,* August 1975, p. 167.

13. The following study was conducted by Judith A. Reisman, Ph.D., in "The Role of Pornography and Media Violence in Family Violence, Sexual Abuse and Exploitation, and Juvenile Delinquency," The American University School of Education, Washington, D.C., 1985.

14. Judith A. Reisman, Testimony before the United States Attorney General's Commission on Pornography, Miami, Florida, 21 November, 1985.

15. *Public Opinion,* Oct./Nov. 1985, p. 38.

16. Robert J. Ringer, *Looking Out For #1,* Fawcett Crest, N.Y., 1977, p. 20.

17. Ringer, p. 325.

18. Ringer, p. 326.

19. Onalee McGraw, "The Family, Feminism and the Therapeutic State," Heritage Foundation Critical Issues Series, 1980, p. 2.

20. Marguerite Michaels, "Who's Raising Our Children?", *Parade Magazine,* 14 July, 1985.

21. Thomas Ricks, "New Minority of Mothers at Home Finds Support in Family Centers," *Wall Street Journal,* 25 October, 1985.

22. Editorial, "Who's Watching the Kids?", *New York Times,* 12 July, 1985.

23. Michaels.

24. Ricks.

25. Shirley Wilkins and Thomas A. W. Miller, "Working Women: How It's Working Out," *Public Opinion,* Oct./Nov. 1985, p. 47.

26. *Richmond Times Dispatch,* 14 April, 1985.

27. *USA Today,* 26 July, 1985.

28. *Richmond Times Dispatch,* 2 September, 1984.

29. Peter Francese, "One-parent Families Growing," *Richmond Times Dispatch,* 22 July, 1984.

30. Francese.

31. Francese.

32. Francese.

33. McGraw, p. 24.

34. *Richmond Times,* 14 April, 1985.

35. *Washington Times,* 26 July, 1985.

36. *USA Today,* 25 February, 1985.

37. *USA Today,* 25 February, 1985.

38. Peter Francese, "Family Stability is Low," *Richmond Times,* 18 August, 1985.

Chapter 8: Fighting Back

1. Sergeant Samuel Alberti, interview with author, 19 March, 1984.

2. Lee Laster, interview with author, 7 March, 1984.

3. William Von Raab, Testimony before the Permanent Subcommittee on Investigations of the Senate Committee on Governmental Affairs, U.S. Senate, 29 November, 1984.

4. *Ibid.*

5. *Ibid.*

6. Walter O'Mally, interview with author, 7 January, 1985.

7. U.S. Customs Service Paper Summarizing Current Cases, August 1984.

8. From U.S. Customs records, Chicago, Ill.

9. *USA Today,* 6 April, 1984.

10. *The Washington Post,* 28 August, 1985.

11. *Washington Times,* 19 July, 1985.

12. *USA Today,* 17 July, 1984.

13. *USA Today,* 19 July, 1985.

14. *Richmond Times,* 28 December, 1985.

15. Dr. Fred S. Berlin, unpublished article entitled, "Medical Aspects of Human Sexuality."

16. The following statements and positions taken by Dr. Fred S. Berlin were reported in: *The Washington Post,* 10 August, 1985; Fred S. Berlin and Genevieve S. Coyle, *The Johns Hopkins Medical Journal,* 9 March, 1981; Fred S. Berlin and Carl F. Meinecke, *American Journal of Psychiatry,* "Treatment of Sex Offenders with Anti-adrogenic Medication," May 1981; Fred S. Berlin, unpublished article entitled, "Medical Aspects of Human Sexuality."

17. *Newsweek,* 1 October, 1984.